INSTRUCTOR'S MANUAL

to accompany

RHOADS MURPHEY

A HISTORY OF ASIA

Second Edition

Michael J. Harvey
Michael G. Murdock

HarperCollins*CollegePublishers*

Instructor's Manual to accompany Rhoads Murphey, *A History of Asia,* second edition.

Copyright © 1996 HarperCollins College Publishers

HarperCollins® and ®® are registered trademarks of HarperCollins Publishers Inc.

All rights reserved. Printed in the United States of America. No part of this book may be used or reproduced in any manner whatsoever without written permission. For information, address HarperCollins College Publishers, 10 East 53rd Street, New York, NY 10022. *For information about any HarperCollins title, product, or resource, please visit our World Wide Web site at* ***http://www.harpercollins.com/college***.

ISBN: 0-673-55826-6

95 96 97 98 99 9 8 7 6 5 4 3 2 1

CONTENTS

The First Day of Class		1
Introduction Monsoon Asia as a Unit of Study		2
1.	Prehistoric Asia	4
2.	The Civilization of Ancient India	10
3.	The Civilization of Ancient China	20
4.	Asian Religions and Their Cultures	30
5.	Medieval India and Southeast Asia	39
6.	China and Korea: A Golden Age	47
7.	Early, Classical, and Medieval Japan	56
8.	Mughal India and Central Asia	64
9.	New Imperial Splendor in China: The Ming Dynasty	72
10.	The Traditional and Early Modern Societies of Asia	80
11.	The West Arrives in Asia	88
12.	Manchu China and Tokugawa Japan	98
13.	The Rise of British Power in India	107
14.	The Triumph of Imperialism in Asia	119
15.	Subjugation, Nationalism, and Revolution in China and India	131
16.	The Struggle for Asia, 1920-1945	142
17.	Revival and Revolution in Japan and China	154
18.	Korea and Southeast Asia in the Modern World	165
19.	South Asia: Independence, Political Division, and Development	176
20.	Asia at the Close of the Century	186
Answer Section		191

PREFACE

As we realize that most instructors will have some academic background on at least one country or region of Asia, but may not be learned in all regions and time periods, this instructor's manual assumes that the instructor possesses little or no knowledge of the subject.

We hope this manual will help instructors use *A History of Asia* to its full potential by allowing them to teach varying countries or regions as semesters/years progress (i.e., South Asia one semester/year, East Asia the next, or all of ancient Asia and then the modern era).

Each chapter of this instructor's manual is divided into four sections:

1. **Outline of Main Ideas.** This section identifies primary ideas, figures and events contained in the respective *A History of Asia* chapter. After reading the chapter, the chapter outlines can provide a review of key points.

2. **Essay and Discussion Questions.** These questions are intended to provide instructors with supplemental information about certain topics for discussion and/or stimulate students interested in further research. Students may be challenged by these questions and they may lead them to analyze various historical elements in persuasive essay or debate-style formats.

3. **Questions for Class Discussion**. These questions may be used in class discussion and/or exam format. Basic answers can be gleaned from the text but may be supplemented by additional research or in the course of discussion between students.

4. **Multiple Choice Questions**. The multiple choice questions have been designed for use in testing or for reading quizzes. They emphasize basic factual recognition and analysis.

Acknowledgments

Michael Harvey would like to thank Professor Murphey for giving his time and skills as his mentor, and for his confidence in allowing him to help with this manual. The scholars who have helped him at different stages are Professors Harold Pinkham, Michael I. Prochilio, and Bryce Eiman. He would like to give great thanks and much love to his family, and to the three he is forever indebted to and will miss always, he dedicates this book to Eleanor, Barbara, and Tom Harvey. He extends his best wishes to the PHS IB classes of 1996 and 1997 and all his past and future students.

Michael G. Murdock wishes to offer his special thanks to Dr. Murphey for his support and impassioned commitment to sharing his knowledge of Asia. He would also like to thank Mari, Mark and Junne for keeping him entertained during this endeavor, and Setsu, whose insightful contributions deserve honorable mention.

Both authors would both like to thank Jessica Bayne at HarperCollins, Dr. Martin Roberts for all his work and expertise, and lastly Josh Davidson, an outstanding young scholar, for his help in this project.

THE FIRST DAY OF CLASS

Questions For Class Discussion

- What do you know about Asia?
- What are some of your first impressions of (list a few countries)?
- Why were these your first impressions? What do they say about you?

Introduction to the Different Geographical Regions of Asia

- *South Asia*: India, Pakistan, Bangladesh, Sri Lanka, Nepal, Bhutan
- *East Asia*: China, Japan, North and South Korea, Taiwan
- *Peninsular Southeast Asia*: Vietnam, Cambodia, Laos, Thailand, Myanmar (Burma). (Geographically, Myanmar is part of South Asia, but culturally it is grouped with Southeast Asia.)
- *Island Southeast Asia*: Malaysia, Indonesia, Philippines.
- *Northern/Central Asia*: Mongolia along with the peoples of the Western regions of China and those with Asian ties living in the former Soviet Union

INTRODUCTION
Monsoon Asia as a Unit of Study

It is imperative that students understand the significance of the monsoon. The majority of Asians work in agriculture and the rains mean survival.

Questions For Class Discussion

1. Why do people celebrate the coming of the monsoon rains?

    People are known to dance in the streets at the arrival of the monsoons not only because the rains are vitally important to agriculture, and thus life itself, but also because in some places they are notoriously unreliable.

2. What are some of the social similarities of monsoon Asia?

    In general the cultures of monsoon Asia tend to distrust individualism and emphasize group effort and welfare. Most Asians place a high value on education and family networks.

Multiple Choice Questions

1. Which of the following is not one of the Western borders of Asia?
    a. The Suez Canal
    b. The Persian Gulf
    c. The Ural Mountains
    d. The Bosphorus at Istanbul

2. The "Summer Monsoon" does not effect:
   a. India.
   b. Burma.
   c. Indonesia.
   d. Thailand.

3. The "Winter Monsoon" supplies rain for:
   a. China.
   b. Vietnam.
   c. Pakistan.
   d. Java.

4. The first Asian civilizations began:
   a. in and around river valleys.
   b. in the mountains.
   c. on the coast.
   d. in the southern island regions.

5. Which of the following is not a marginal region of China?
   a. Tibet
   b. Mongolia
   c. Bhutan
   d. Sinkiang

6. Which of the following is not a sub-region of monsoon Asia?
   a. Japan
   b. India
   c. China
   d. Siberia

7. Population densities in Asia are generally:
   a. high.
   b. low.
   c. about the same as those of the West.
   d. low except for those of China.

CHAPTER 1
Prehistoric Asia

Outline of Main Ideas

A. Early and Paleolithic Cultures
- *homo erectus; homo neanderthalis; homo sapiens*; regional physical differences; early culture: fire, weapons, cave paintings; early adaptation to environmental changes

B. The Neolithic Revolution
- the emergence of the elements of civilization; "neolithic" as a stage of development; early cradles of civilization and the advent of agriculture and the domestication of animals; Indus Valley settlements; irrigation; metalwork; the spread of agricultural technology and the growth of cities

C. Agricultural Origins in Southeast Asia
- the origins of rice; the role of root crops; Hoabinhian culture; other possible sites of early cultures; the origins of domesticated animals; the role of millet

D. Peoples and Early Kingdoms of Southeast Asia
- early migrations; the Malays and movements south; southern Chinese and their migrations further south; the spread of mainland Southeast Asian culture into south China; the spread of technology and culture; early kingdoms in mainland Southeast Asia: Funan, Champa, Vietnamese, Burmese at Pagan; the Thais, the Khmer

E. Malaya, Indonesia, and the Philippines
- the Malayan principalities; Srivijaya and Indian culture; the tribal societies of the Philippines

F. Prehistoric China
- heavy southern Chinese influence in the north; the climate of north China: loess; pottery, millet; Pan P'o village; irrigation; Yang Shao (Painted Pottery) culture; Lung Shan (Black Pottery) Culture; bronze, walled towns; the similarities between Lung Shan culture and the Shang dynasty; the independent development of Chinese civilization

G. Korea and Japan
- the spread of millet-based agriculture into Korea from north China; the origins of the Korean people; the traditional origins of the Korean people; iron; Choson; the Han conquest of Korea; Chinese colonies and influence
- Japanese isolation and identity; the origins of the Japanese people; Japan's earliest inhabitants—Jomon culture; Yayoi culture and its connections to China; the appearance of the "Japanese" and iron culture
- Chinese accounts of Japan; the Kojiki ("Record of Ancient Matters") and Nihongi ("History of Japan"); the creation myths; the Yamato state and its emperor; Shinto; early links with Korea and China; slow migrations northeast from Kyushu; the introduction of Buddhism and the Chinese model

Essay And Discussion Questions

1. What does the term "neolithic" refer to?
   The term "neolithic," which literally means "New Stone Age" does not specify a period of time. Rather, it describes a particular stage of development. Technologically, it is characterized by a greater use of stone implements, the extensive utilization of bone and pottery implements and the gradual development of metalworking technology and its use for tools and weapons. Large permanent settlements and even cities begin to appear along with great increases in population based on the agricultural surplus of established agrarian communities.

   Associated with towns and cities, urban culture begins. Writing develops, often associated with a ruling class or religious elites for the purpose of keeping records, recording transactions or communicating with the gods. Religious rites become associated with leadership and classes begin to form. In short, the essentials of civilization develop and shape society.

2. What impact did the ancient south China and/or mainland Southeast Asian cultures have on north China?
   In general most Chinese and Western accounts of Chinese civilization emphasize the Yellow River Valley and the North China Plain as the birthplace of Chinese civilization. The heavy northern emphasis in traditional renderings of the development of Chinese civilization can be attributed to both the dry northern climate, which preserves archeological artifacts better for longer, and the political dominance of the northern Chinese and their eagerness to substantiate their own import by identifying "Chinese civilization" with northern civilization.

   Recently, however, scholars have begun to shift their attention southward in an effort to fill in our understanding of China's early roots. Some scholars now credit the south with the first developments of agriculture in China saying it only later spread to the north. Other agrarian developments, such as the domestication of pigs, chickens, and the water buffalo certainly originated in the south and spread north. Wet rice agriculture also moved north, as most likely did bronze technology and metalworking. Today, these elements constitute the basics of agrarian life throughout East Asia.

Questions For Class Discussion

1. What archaeological evidence exists to suggest that a large and expansive group of people lived in Southeast Asia from 4500 BCE to 2000 BCE?
   Bronze tools, weapons, and millet requiring cultivation are the strongest evidence to date. Along with this evidence are the remains of domesticated pigs and chickens.

2. Though Southeast Asia has a distinct culture, it continues to share much with both China (foods, language, social culture) and India (Burmese and Thai written languages and political kingdoms). How did this blending of culture occur?
   The geographical locations of China and India in relation to Southeast Asia had much to do with the blending of cultural trends in Southeast Asia. The close proximity of these three areas opened the door to trade and occasional warfare. More exchanges between Southeast Asia, India, and China will be discussed in future chapters.

3. Why are finds of pottery fragments important? What do they tell us about China?
   Pottery itself tells archaeologists much concerning a society's fortunes, and storage requirements for surpluses. The intricacy of design shows relative advances or

declines of a civilization. Pottery of high quality and decorational complexity tends to identify a civilization that is prosperous enough to warrant such work.

4. What impact did Chinese culture and civilization have on Korea? Why?
China probably influenced the founding of Korea, its iron technology, and many cultural similarities. However, the Korean language developed independently. China seldom controlled Korea outright, but was often able to maintain at least a hegemonic relationship with the smaller nation. Chinese influence remained heavy, particularly during much of the Han dynasty (109 BCE to CE 220) and then again from the seventh to the eighteenth centuries.

Multiple Choice Questions

1. The oldest ancestor of modern man to be found in Asia has been located in both:
   a. Java and China.
   b. India and China.
   c. Vietnam and Java.
   d. India and Burma.

2. The Neolithic Revolution began:
   a. 150,000 years ago.
   b. 3,000 years ago.
   c. about 10,000 years ago.
   d. 20,000 years ago.

3. Which of the following was not an innovation of the Neolithic Revolution?
   a. Improved tool making
   b. Farming
   c. Printing
   d. Pottery

4. Loess is:
   a. silt from rivers.
   b. coastal sand.
   c. clay deposits.
   d. rich layers of dust blown by glacial winds.

5. Rice farming began in:
   a. Southeast Asia.
   b. China.
   c. Japan.
   d. India.

6. Most of the inhabitants of modern Southeast Asia originally came from:
   a. India.
   b. China.
   c. Japan.
   d. Java.

7. The first Indonesian state of which we have detailed knowledge is:
   a. Java.
   b. Srivijaya.
   c. Hoabinhian.
   d. Funan.

8. Thus far, the emergence of civilization in China is best documented:
   a. along the Yellow River.
   b. on the coast.
   c. in Manchuria.
   d. in Yunan.

9. Probably the earliest crop to be farmed in North China was:
   a. rice.
   b. wheat.
   c. barley.
   d. millet.

10. Among the pre-dynastic cultures of China was the:
    a. Jomon culture.
    b. Lung Shan culture.
    c. Yayoi culture.
    d. Hoabinhian culture.

11. Japan's earliest neolithic culture was the:
    a. Han.
    b. Hoabinhian.
    c. Jomon.
    d. Yin.

12. The Kojiki and the Nihongi are:
    a. early Chinese histories.
    b. ancient texts of Japan.
    c. Jomon pottery styles.
    d. histories of Korea.

13. The Straits of Tsushima separate:
    a. China from Japan.
    b. India from Sri Lanka.
    c. Japan from Russia.
    d. Japan from Korea.

CHAPTER 2
The Civilization of Ancient India

Outline Of Main Ideas

India. The oldest surviving civilization; a brief outline of ancient India

A. Origins of Civilization in India
- the appearance of cities in various cultures around the globe; the term "civilization"; links between India and Sumer (Egypt); agriculture, irrigation and real cities

B. The Indus Civilization
- the Indus River and surrounding city sites; the Indus' geography and its comparability to Sumer; irrigation and agriculture

    i. Relations with Sumer
    - the undeciphered nature and independent origins of the script; distinct art and city planning; seals as facilitators of trade; problems with Indus archeology; the name of the civilization?; trade with Sumer

    ii. The Cities of the Indus
    - city layout; the apparent emphasis on bathing and water; religious artifacts; buildings and structures; art, toys, cotton, seals; wheat and agricultural crops; irrigation efforts; bricks

    iii. Decline and Fall
- signs of decay and violence; ecological problems; irrigation-related problems; migrations; the Aryans

C. The Aryans
- the term "Aryan"; the Aryans and their early culture; early historical accounts; Vedic period culture; the relationship of Sanskrit to European languages

    i. Aryan Domination
- Aryan chariots and military might; Aryan accounts of their deeds; the beginnings of caste?; Aryan verses Dravidian culture, mutual influence and spheres of influence

    ii. Vedic Culture
- the rise of traditional Indian culture; Indian medicine, industry, and science; the impact of Vedic culture on the West

D. The Rise of Empire: Mauryan India
- development in the Ganges River valley

    i. The Invasion of Alexander the Great
- the conquest of West Punjab; Alexander's cosmopolitan mission; Greek impact on and Greek curiosity in India

E. The Maurya Dynasty
- Chandragupta; the Arthashastra and power politics; Chinese Legalism; the breakup of older socio-political institutions; the Book of Megasthenes

    i. Pataliputra and the Glory of Mauryan India
- Pataliputra and its grandeur; state enterprises and institutions; prosperity and wealth; maritime trade; extensive transport networks

    ii. The Emperor Ashoka, "Beloved of the Gods"
- Bindusara; the British rediscovery of Ashoka; Ashoka's campaigns south; the conquest of righteousness; Buddhism; all people as Ashoka's "children"; softer and gentler rule; Buddhist missions to Southeast Asia

F. Kushans and Greeks
   - civil war; nomadic invaders; the Kushans; Indianization; the legacy of Buddhist sculpture; Indian-Greek trade and intercourse of ideas; Christianity in India; Periplus of the Erythrean Sea

G. Southern India and the City of Madurai
   - the rich civilizations of the south; competing states; Madurai and depictions of urban life there

H. Ceylon
   - Ceylon's distinct culture and identity; Prince Vijaya and the Sinhalese; the Veddas; extensive agriculture and irrigation; Anuradhapura and state control; Buddhism and its massive stupas; Ceylon's interaction with India; the Tamils; the Chola invasion and Polonnaruwa; further invasion and the decline of Ceylon's irrigation systems

I. The Guptas and the Empire of Harsha
   - the Gupta dynasty at Pataliputra; contact with Southeast Asia; Chinese accounts

   i. Life and Culture in the Guptan Period
      - peaceful and mild rule; the blossoming of Sanskrit literature; monumental building; Kalidasa

   ii. The Collapse of the Guptas
      - invasion by the White Huns; Indian contact with the West; India's isolation from China; chaos and regionalization; the rise of Harsha

J. Women in Ancient India
   - Vedic India: matriarchal society; women and power, property and status; women and the arts, philosophy, religion; goddesses
   - Mauryan India: the reduced scope of women; greater restrictions; Gupta India: even greater restrictions
   - courtesans, their status and freedom; hereditary dancers; sati

K. The Indian Heritage
- regionalization and cultural diversity; India's similarities with Europe; the value of regionalization?; respect for education; village life and relative well-being; scientific and medical contributions

Essay And Discussion Questions

1. What led to the decline of the Indus Valley Civilization?
   While we may never know the particulars, the peoples of the Indus Valley seem to have encountered an ecological and agricultural crisis that dried up their supplies of food. Salts and other alkalines remaining in the soil after decades of irrigation and evaporation without sufficient rainfall to wash them away probably destroyed the soil's ability to grow crops. Similarly, rising water tables can ruin fields by drowning the roots of crops. It may also be that changes in the course of the river as silt filled up the river bed, forcing water to find another course to the sea, also had catastrophic affects on cities dependent upon the now distant river.

   While their technology allowed the Indus Valley inhabitants to thrive for a time, they were ultimately unable to deal with ecological changes which deprived them of their food supply, weakening them and making them vulnerable to invaders.

2. What effects did ancient Indian civilization have on the West?

   While volumes could be written in answer to this question, a few highlights can serve to represent the rest. Indian advances in medicine spread to Greece where it was welcomed and adopted. Likewise, mathematics, including the so-called Arabic system, and steel manufacturing technology first spread to the Arabs before arriving in the West. Also, Greek assumptions about the natural order of the universe probably stemmed from the Indian concept of Rta.
   Accompanying the conquests of Alexander the Great and his burning desire to fuse Eastern and Western cultures, the flow of culture, religion, and technology increased rapidly. Indian philosophy received not only attention from Greek philosophers, but from Alexander himself who sought meetings with India's renowned sages. Extensive and long-lived trade networks between India and the West regularly ushered Greek merchants back and forth, providing an avenue for greater cultural exchange. Indian philosophers even visited the Mediterranean and Leventine cities perhaps contributing

to the intellectual heritage of the West. Unfortunately, India often does not often get credit for its contributions because Indians did little to preserve their own history.

Questions For Class Discussion

1. Why were the first centers of Indian civilization situated around the Indus river valley? It is the first major river to which the settlers from Sumer would have most likely migrated. Although the surrounding area is basically desert, the Indus' river water and fertile silt provide excellent irrigation and soil for farming. The river also offers the easy transport necessary for trade.

2. What reasons can be given to account for the peaceful and prosperous rule of Ashoka? The strong centralized cultural center of Pataliputra allowed the government to maintain administrative control over a diverse empire. However, through humane means and visionary actions, rather than apartheid or ethnic cleansing, the regime was able to establish a system satisfactory to most of these diverse groups.

3. What does India's later history as "separate regional kingdoms" say about the chances of modern day India succeeding as a whole?
This question is for advanced and/or politically astute students. This question can be used again in Chapter 19.

   Pakistan separated from India in 1949. East Pakistan broke off from Pakistan and became independent as Bangladesh in 1971. Fighting has continued between different groups seeking independence since the 1960's (i.e. Sikhs in the Punjab, Muslims in Kashmir). History, ancient and modern, seems to indicate that unity will be difficult. Note that Ashoka's Kingdom (see map p.24) remains the largest and most unified in the history of the Indian Subcontinent.

4. War is sometimes called "the mother of invention" yet it is also remarkably destructive. What evidence does the text provide that indicates that sometimes the latter assertion makes the prior one irrelevant? (This question and the next can be used throughout this text.)
As Tamil raids increased, civil war destroyed the irrigation works and thus destroyed the basis of Sri Lanka society. Today's Sri Lankan civil war is once again destroying a society. Also, the invasion of Alexander the Great certainly weakened the societies in the Northwest Frontier although it did not completely destroy them.

5. Invasions have meant death and destruction in India (and everywhere else). Nevertheless, one might argue that some positive developments have also resulted from the invasions. What might some of the advantages be?
It can be argued that an accelerated and more advanced mixture of cultures is an advantage to both parties, though trade and other more peaceful means may accomplish the same result. Some may argue that an invading force brought with it a superior culture such as the Hellenistic ways of Alexander. This should lead to an interesting class discussion.

6. Why might ancient India be described as an island with a causeway?
Except for the Khyber pass, travel by land into India is very difficult.

7. Why are the writings of the Chinese important to historians of other Asian civilizations?
Chinese writings give historians the best (and sometimes only) written record about an ancient civilization. Thus, the writings of Chinese travelers such as Fa Hsien or Hsuan Tsang to Gupta period India provide our only glimpse of that culture. Similarly, Chinese writings about ancient Korea and Japan offer unique insight.

8. What arguments could Indian women of today draw from ancient India to support calls for more equality?
Students should recognize that traditions are constantly changing. In early periods, Indian women had great social influence and wider social roles. Many Indian gods were women and even the Mahabharata (see p.40), a very important religious text, praised women.

Multiple Choice Questions

1. Indian civilization is thought to have begun in:
   a. the Ganges Valley.
   b. the Deccan.
   c. Kashmir.
   d. the Indus Valley.

2. Which of the following was not a major urban center of Indus Valley civilization?
    a. Harrapa
    b. Delhi
    c. Mohenjo Daro
    d. Kalibangan

3. The head-waters of the Indus River begin their journey in:
    a. the Himalaya Mountains.
    b. the Deccan Plateau.
    c. the Hindu Kush.
    d. the Satpura Mountains.

4. Indus Valley civilization traded with:
    a. Crete.
    b. China.
    c. Sumer.
    d. Bengal.

5. Cotton weaving probably began in:
    a. China.
    b. Southeast Asia.
    c. Sumer.
    d. the Indus Valley civilization.

6. The chief Indus food crop was:
    a. millet.
    b. wheat.
    c. barley.
    d. rice.

7. The Aryans invaded India from:
    a. Europe.
    b. China.
    c. South Central Asia.
    d. the Deccan.

8. The Mahabharata and the Ramayana are:
   a. Aryan ritual books.
   b. Aryan epic poems.
   c. Aryan hymns of creation.
   d. Aryan histories.

9. The language of the Vedic period was:
   a. Tamil.
   b. Hindi.
   c. Sanskrit.
   d. Dravidian.

10. Aryan civilization was centered in:
    a. Sri Lanka.
    b. Southern India.
    c. the Deccan.
    d. Northern India.

11. The first detailed reports of Vedic culture came from:
    a. Egyptian merchants.
    b. the Greeks of Alexander the Great's army.
    c. Chinese historians.
    d. Herodotus.

12. By 500 B.C.E. the center of Indian civilization had shifted to:
    a. the Indus Valley.
    b. the Deccan.
    c. the Ganges Valley.
    d. Kashmir.

13. Porus:
    a. stopped Alexander's advance into India
    b. founded the Mauryan Dynasty.
    c. conquered the Deccan.
    d. became a Greek ally.

14. The founder of the Mauryan Dynasty was:
    a. Porus.
    b. Arjuna.
    c. Hananan.
    d. Chandragupta.

14. Pataliputra was:
    a. the capital of the Mauryan Empire.
    b. the great rival of the Mauryan Empire.
    c. the second Mauryan ruler.
    d. a Greek kingdom in Northern India.

16. The first of the Mauryan rulers was:
    a. Chandragupta.
    b. Porus.
    c. Bindusara.
    d. Ashoka.

17. During the later part of Ashoka's life he devoted himself largely to:
    a. conquest.
    b. putting down rebellions.
    c. spreading Buddhism.
    d. practicing the arts.

18. After Ashoka's death the Mauryan dynasty was replaced by that of the:
    a. Sakas.
    b. Kushans.
    c. Guptas.
    d. Chen.

19. We have evidence of Roman trade with:
    a. the Mauryan dynasty.
    b. the Kushan dynasty.
    c. the Harrapan cities.
    d. the Vedic Empire.

20. A major geographical barrier to the invasion of Southern India was:
    a. the Deccan Plateau.
    b. the Indus Valley.
    c. the Ganges River.
    d. the Satapura Mountains.

21. Which of the following was not a state in Southern India?
    a. Chola
    b. Bengal
    c. Pandya
    d. Pallava

22. The Garland of Madurai is an account of:
    a. the creation of the world.
    b. the defeat of the Mauryans.
    c. an Indian love poem.
    d. life in ancient South India.

23. The first Aryan ruler of Sri Lanka was:
    a. Ashoka.
    b. Pandava.
    c. Kurasa.
    d. Vijaya.

24. Ceylon was the:
    a. birthplace of Buddhism.
    b. first place outside of India to accept Buddhism.
    c. last bastion of Hinduism.
    d. center of Vedic culture.

CHAPTER 3
The Civilization of Ancient China

Outline Of Main Ideas

China: the independent development of Chinese culture; China's continuous and thus slow changing tradition; two millennia of development; the Chinese model of civilization and the Sinitic world

A. The Origins of China
- Lung Shan culture; walled cities; bronze; early forms of pictographic script; silk production
- the Shang Dynasty; the consolidation of Yang Shao and Lung Shan cultures; the as of yet uncorroborated Hsia Dynasty; oracle bones and corroboration of the Shang Dynasty; early cities; mythical cultural heroes; elements of Chinese culture from the west, elements from the south; southern verses northern culture; little contact with the West

B. The Shang Dynasty
- agricultural products; hunting; domesticated animals; slaves; Anyang and other large cities; the royal tombs and their contents; oracle bones and the lifestyles of the Shang elites; productive agriculture

C. The Chou Dynasty
- slave revolts and rebellion; the fall of the Shang Dynasty; the Chou conquest; continuation of Shang culture; the Chou's revision of history; the "Mandate of Heaven"; the Chou's feudal-like political system based on mutual defense

concerns; serfdom; technological and artistic development in urban areas; inscriptions and writing; early classics
- iron tools and agricultural production; urbanization and specialized occupations; increasing trade and social mobility

    i   The Warring States
- the move to Loyang; the Ch'in as guardians against barbarian invasion; dissolution of central authority; rivalry between great vassal states; the spread of technology; the State of Ch'u: trade, naval power, a sophisticated central government; the nature of warfare; the gradual weakening of the Chou system

    ii. Confucius the Sage
- background; the overwhelming success of his philosophy; the Analects; education and morale example; social harmony from within, not without; benevolent government; the superior man

D. The Ch'in Conquest
- the strength and rise of Ch'in; Ch'in strategies and enemy weaknesses; the Ch'in unification of China; the establishment of the imperial system; efforts to consolidate power and centralize control; the Great Wall and other projects

    i. Ch'in Authoritarianism
- Ch'in censorship of merchants, aristocrats and intellectuals; the book burnings; Legalism; Li Ssu and state control; China's propensity for unification; denial of the individual; the advantages of unity; the example of Li Ping

E. The Han Dynasty
- rebellion and the fall of Ch'in; civil war; Liu Pang and the Han Dynasty; retention of the Ch'in system; Han Legalism softened with common sense Confucianism; government to serve the people; the "people of Han"

    i. Expansion under Han Wu-ti
- hands-off government; Han Wu-ti and centralization; militarization and conquest; the Silk Road; the defeat of the Hsiung-nu barbarians; garrisons and watch towers

ii. China and Rome
- limited direct contact; Chang Ch'ien; merchants in Rome; Roman views of China; the role of Central Asians as middlemen; Han Wu-ti's apology; abandonment of campaigns

iii. Wider Trade Patterns
- the importance of intracontinental trade; failure of East-West direct contact; the transmission of ideas along trade networks; Chinese exports to Central Asia and then the Mediterranean; silk, porcelain; lacquer; India

iv. Han Culture
- Han China's flourishing arts; Confucianism; the civil service exam; the success of the Confucian system; Wang Mang's reforms for increased central control and peasant relief; gentry interests and Wang's murder
- the Eastern Han Dynasty in Loyang; prosperity; Pan Ch'ao in Sinkiang; landlordism and stratification; court factionalism and intrigue; central weakness; regionalization; the crumbling of Han order and control

v. The Collapse of the Han Order
- division of China into three rival states; barbarian conquests in the north; four centuries of chaos; Buddhism; the hope of unity

vi. Cities in Ancient China
- cities as symbolic centers of royal authority; city walls; inner verses outer inhabitants; the planned inner city verses the unplanned outer city; Ch'ang An: orientation and layout; the construction of walled cities elsewhere

vii. Han Achievements
- technological and scientific advancements; the reconstruction of lost texts; the sophisticated recording of history

Essay And Discussion Questions

1.) What did the Chou dynasty hope to accomplish by writing a history of the deposed Shang dynasty court?
Throughout Chinese history, establishing a moral claim to power has been an issue of supreme importance to all political regimes. Political or military power, while critical

to seizing power, generally proved insufficient to govern with once power had been taken. In fact, China's most powerful militaristic dynasties, the Qin, the Sui and the Mongols, also proved to be the shortest dynasties because they failed to establish a clear moral claim to the throne.

By writing a history of the Shang court that carefully explicated the crimes and excesses of the regime, the Chou leadership sought to justify its own actions to the rest of China and to subsequent generations. The Shang regime, they reasoned, neglected its responsibilities, abused its power, sapped China's resources and thus lost the support of Heaven. The Chou, on the other hand, portrayed themselves as possessing gifted and compassionate leadership incapable of such follies. Also depicted were many auspicious portents indicating that Heaven had turned its blessing away from the Shang and toward the Chou. Finally, the fact that the Chou succeeded in routing the Shang and supplanting it served as a clear indication that Heaven indeed was watching over their actions.

This Heavenly blessing, in short, provided the Chou with their moral claim to the throne. "Heaven is with us, who can be against us." The significant part of all this, however, and the part that distinguishes ancient Chinese politics from that of other civilizations is that Heaven's blessing is predicated on one's "virtue" and compassionate disposition as opposed to one's birthright. Unlike the British or Japanese emperors or kings who become such by being born into the right family, the Chinese emperor or king has to prove his "virtue" and moral right to the throne. If the leader's virtue became questionable, he became vulnerable to attacks on his legitimacy.

2. In what ways did the Ch'in dynasty "unify" China?

The Ch'in brought most of China as we know it today under the control of one central government, thus unifying the country politically. However, the extent to which unification extended far exceeded simple political unification. By the end of the Warring States period, the various states had been separated politically for hundreds of years. Each had distinctive cultures, dialects, and sociopolitical systems. They all used their own forms of coinage, weights and measures, legal codes, customs and rituals, etc. The states even utilized different written characters.

The Ch'in conquest marked the beginning of the end of much of this diversity by imposing on all of China a system of uniformity and conformity. All legal systems and codes were scrapped and replaced by the Ch'in code. All other writing, measuring and monetary systems met the same fate. History books except for those dealing with Ch'in history were burned as were any books that had no "practical" usage while individuals protesting the book burnings often lost their lives.

The Ch'in also made efforts to tie China together and integrate the different regions so they would function as parts of "China" rather than independent regions. Broad roads connected all major regions of the empire. A postal service for imperial use allowed the capital to communicate with all points in the empire. Old state boundaries were eliminated as China was divided into provinces to be overseen by governors appointed by the central government. Wealthy families in the various regions, which might serve as alternative nodes of power, were uprooted and forced to move to the capital where the emperor could keep an eye on them. In short, the Ch'in demanded unity and conformity at all levels, from the width of the roads to the thoughts in people's heads, as the imperial government attempted to create a polity greater than the sum of the parts.

(3) The Han dynasty chose to use the Ch'in legalist system instead of returning to feudalism. How did they change it to make it more palatable to the population?
In its pure form, Legalism sought to limit education in order to keep people simple and thus more exploitable and less able to rebel. It also restricted travel, thought, scholarly and commercial activity, music, literature and art, and imposed upon society very high taxes and harsh legal codes to extract all possible resources from society for state use. Naturally, many found the Ch'in system to be repressive and dreary.

The Han, recognized some of the positive elements of Legalism and incorporated them into the Han sociopolitical system: including the division of China into provinces headed by centrally-appointed governors, the empire-wide road and canal networks, the uniformity of the written language, weights, measures, coinage, etc. and the central imperial government system itself. To the relief of the people, however, other elements were quickly discarded, such as the harsh legal codes and punishments, heavy taxes, bans on education and culture, bans on commercial activity, etc.

Most importantly, the Han introduced Confucianism's "rule by virtue" as the standard by which government assessed successful or unsuccessful administration. Educated men trained in good books were brought into government service to insure that the "best of men" provided China with benevolent and competent leadership. Thus,

Chinese government became "paternal" in that the government now claimed to serve the people in return for their loyalty and support.

Questions For Class Discussion

1. What impact did technological improvements have on Chou Dynasty feudalism?
   The technological improvements brought increased agricultural production, which allowed for more people to become involved in non-agricultural pursuits, such as trade. The growth of cities which followed led to feudalism's obsolescence.

2. Do you agree "that people can be molded and elevated by education?"
   Answers will vary, of course. Make sure students define "molded" and "elevated" in their own terms. If they answer "no", then they might be asked why they attend class.

3. Continue the previous question: Can people "be molded and elevated by education and by the virtuous example of superiors?"
   A definition of "superiors" is needed. If the students answer "yes", they might be asked why they do not listen to their teachers, parents, and clergy more often? If the students answer "no", invite them to take over the class. Some may say that we are all equal, thus having no superiors: this is an interesting proposal that should spark good discussion from all sides.

4. According to Mencius does your government practice "good government"? Is his definition of good government a useful one?

5. Comment on Mo-tzu's assertion in Reflections that a prince is unjust to glorify war but call murder a crime?

6. Professor Murphey asks "Are people better off forcefully unified in an empire at tremendous cost in lives than if they had been left to their own regional cultures and states?" How would you answer this question?
   Answers will vary, but for those who say "no", it may be useful to raise examples of attempts by governments to change people's religion, cultural norms and expressions, social standings, livelihood, sexual preference, etc. This subject can easily be used to discuss current events and the history of different regions.

7. Wu Ti was able to stave off a rebellion by promising to be a better ruler. Would you have called for his overthrow?

Multiple Choice Questions

1. The first Chinese dynasty for which we have substantial archaeological evidence is the:
   a. Shang.
   b. Lung Shan.
   c. Hsia.
   d. Yang Shao.

2. The chief crop of Shang China was:
   a. rice.
   b. wheat.
   c. barley.
   d. millet.

3. The culture of Shang China is best known for its:
   a. literature.
   b. conquests.
   c. bronze work.
   d. music.

4. The last great capital of the Shang dynasty was:
   a. Loyang.
   b. Cheng-chou.
   c. Hang-chow.
   d. Anyang.

5. When the Shang dynasty fell it was replaced by the:
   a. Hsia dynasty.
   b. Chou dynasty.
   c. Ch'ing dynasty.
   d. Tang dynasty.

6. The base of Chou power was in:
   a. the Yellow River Basin.
   b. the coastal regions.
   c. the Wei River Valley.
   d. Southern China.

7. One of the great philosophical achievements of Chou China was the:
   a. I-Ching.
   b. Seven Pieces of Brocade.
   c. Book of Lord Shang.
   d. Diamond Sutra.

8. Confucius lived during the late:
   a. Ch'in.
   b. Chou.
   c. Tang.
   d. Han.

9. The most well known architectural achievement of the Ch'in dynasty was:
   a. Anyang.
   b. the Great Wall.
   c. the Grand Canal.
   d. Loyang.

10. Ch'in rule could be characterized as:
    a. lenient.
    b. democratic.
    c. authoritarian.
    d. disorganized.

11. The first emperor of the Ch'in Dynasty was:
    a. Li Ping.
    b. Hsun-tzu.
    c. Li Ssu.
    d. Ch'in Shih Huang Ti.

12. Which of the following figures was not a member of the legalist school of Chinese philosophy?
    a. Li Ssu
    b. Lord Shang
    c. Lao Tze
    d. Han Fei-tzu

13. The founder of the Han dynasty was:
    a. Hsun-tzu.
    b. Liu Pang.
    c. Lord Shang.
    d. Li Ssu.

14. The Han dynasty adopted the ideas of what philosopher to replace the authoritarianism of the Ch'in?
    a. Confucius
    b. Lao Tze
    c. Mencius
    d. Li Ping

15. Han military power reached its peak under the emperor:
    a. Han Kao-tsu.
    b. Li Ping.
    c. Wu Ti.
    d. Tsao Tsao.

16. Rome and the Han dynasty:
    a. were direct trading partners.
    b. were enemies.
    c. knew nothing of each other.
    d. had no direct or regular contact.

17. The route that connected China with the Middle East and ultimately Western Europe was known as the:
    a. Royal Highway.
    b. Silk Road.
    c. Northern Route.
    d. Road of Death.

18. The second period of Han rule in China is known as the:
    a. Lesser Han.
    b. Eastern Han.
    c. Younger Han.
    d. Wang dynasty.

19. The capital of the Han state was:
    a. Anyang.
    b. Yin.
    c. Ch'ang An.
    d. Canton.

CHAPTER 4
Asian Religions and Their Cultures

Outline Of Main Ideas
Asia as the source of major religions

A. Hinduism
   - ancient beginnings; the caste system and jatis

   i. Hindu Beliefs and Writings
      - Hinduism as a combination of Harappan, Aryan, and Dravidian cultures; the Vedas, Upanishads, and Bhagavad Gita; dharma, karma, ahimsa

   ii. Reincarnation
      - reincarnation, samsara, moksha; Vishnu, Shiva and Brahma; the lack of ritual, clergy, etc.; Brahmins; numerous and popular festivals; artha, karma; the acceptance and celebration of good and bad of life

B. Zoroastrianism
   - Zoroaster and his visions; the wandering preacher; Avesta; polytheism; Indra and fire; the importance of light; Ahura-Mazda; judgment; repentance; atonement and remission of sins; the sacred nature of soil, water and fire; the defiling nature of death; Ahriman; the daeva; fire alters and temple sacrifice; the religion's spread with Persian culture into western and central Asia; the Islamic conquests; Bombay today

C. Buddhism in India and Its Spread Eastward
- India's political turmoil and suffering; Buddhism as a reaction against Hindu ritualization and the caste system

   i. Gautama Buddha
   - Gautama's royal background; Gautama's encounter with four types of men, quits the palace and becomes an ascetic; meditation, temptation and enlightenment; Gautama becomes the Buddha; travels and sermons; the Four Noble Truths; nirvana; Tripitaka; the conversion of Emperor Ashoka, Buddhism's spread to southeast Asia; Indian Buddhism's slow reabsorption into Hinduism; the Islamic conquests

   ii. Hinayana and Mahayana Buddhism
   - Hinayana: good works and karma; Hinayana's dominance in Southeast Asia; sincere religious commitment in Southeast Asia today
   - Mahayana: the popularization of Buddhism; Bodhisattvas; good works and salvation; Lamaistic Buddhism; magic; heaven and hell; Buddhism's impact on art
   - Mahayana Buddhism in East Asia; Ch'an (Zen) Buddhism; the suppression of Buddhism in China; the role of Buddhism in Japan today

D. Confucianism
- Confucianism: a moral philosophy?; the impact of Confucianism

   i. Confucius and Mencius
   - Confucius' similarities to Plato; disciples; Mencius

   ii. The Confucian View
   - hierarchy and responsibility; "right relationships," self-cultivation, and education as the path to morality; human goodness via example and education as opposed to force and laws; Confucianism's initial disinterest in metaphysics; the exam system; the mandate of Heaven
   - the humane, this-world nature of Confucianism; leisure and the enjoyment of life verses striving for accumulated wealth; the natural world as a model for the human realm; ancestor worship and the importance of male progeny

- Chu Hsi and neo-Confucianism; Confucianism as a religion?; imperial rites and responsibilities; Confucianism and modern economic growth; individualism and freedom

E. Taoism
- the dominance of the natural world over the human realm; the Tao Te Ching; Lao Tze; the futility of human endeavors; Chuang Tze
- religious Taoism: magic, alchemy, Chinese medicine; the Taoist pantheon; Chinese adherence to both Confucianism and Taoism; yin and yang harmony

F. Judaism in Asia
- Jewish settlements in India, their retention of Hebrew culture and eventual return to Israel; Jewish settlements in T'ang China; the Nestorian Christians; Jewish peoples in Sung and Ming China and their absorption into Chinese culture

G. Islam in Asia
- Mohammed; monotheism; the Koran and commentaries; Islam in India, Southeast, and East Asia; the dispersion of Islam along the trade routes
- beliefs: monotheism, resurrection, heaven, judgment, prayer and salvation, angels and prophets; prayer and muezzin; mullahs; Ramadan; hajj to Mecca and Medina; prohibitions; the status of women; jihad
- the Islamic conquest of the Middle East and north Africa; Islam's entry into India and Southeast Asia; Islam in China and its absorption into Chinese society

H. Shinto
- origins in nature worship; the Japanese religion; no philosophy; emphases on purity and cleansing ritual; kami; purification and bathing; Shinto shrines; Ise; torii gates; worship at Shinto shrines

I. Asian Religions: Some Reflections
- eclecticism and the dominance of Asian religions in Asia; the difficulty of Western missionary work there; Hinduism as Indian culture; Confucianism as a transcultural institution; Buddhism, Christianity and Islam as universal, proselytizing creeds; differing views of evil; misbehavior; redemption; views of the natural world

Essay And Discussion Questions

1. What distinguishes Theravada (or Hinayana) Buddhism from Mahayana Buddhism?
   Perhaps the most obvious distinguishing characteristic between the two branches of Buddhism lays in their geographic distribution. Theravada Buddhism migrated east and achieved dominance in Southeast Asia, particularly Burma, Thailand, Cambodia and Laos where it remains the dominant religion today and continues to exert a great deal of influence on society. Mahayana Buddhism, on the other hand, spread from India into Central Asia and east from there along the Silk Route into China, Korea and Japan. In China, various sects of Mahayana Buddhism remain but only as shadows of the once great Buddhist presence there.

   Doctrinally, Theravada Buddhism emphasizes "good works," such as donating money to construct a temple, as a means to build good karma and offset evil works. Mahayana Buddhism's various sects differ greatly on this point. Some claim salvation comes through faith and appealing to the Buddha with a simple phrase while others demand laborious rituals and still others demand total self-mastery and discipline through self-denial and meditation. Mahayana Buddhism also added a broad pantheon of Buddhas, Bodhisattvas, and attendants in both heaven and the various layers of hell.

2. What are the fundamental difference between Confucianism and Taoism?
   Confucianism and Taoism stem from the same time period and address the same major issue: how can harmony and stability be obtained. Taoism stresses that all creatures and entities within the natural world (humans being no exception) have endowed within them a "destiny" or "way" that they are intended to follow. Following this natural course would bring personal harmony and balance with the rest of the natural world. Since each entity possesses its own personal way, it can follow no other and enter a harmonious relationship with the greater "way" of nature. "Evil" in the world is created when individuals or things are prevented from following the natural courses of their existence. Society and its laws, social expectations, family systems, hierarchies, languages, governments, etc. placed obstacles in the paths of humans by distracting them with ambitions like wealth, fame, power, etc. or by consuming their time and energy with useless efforts (such as building pleasures palaces, walls, prisons, etc.). Society is bad because it allows kings, emperors or elites to impose upon all other beings one particular "way" while denying them the freedom to live their own "way."

The Confucians also claimed that nature endowed each being or entity with a destiny or way and that following that way led to harmony. However the harmony Confucians sought was social harmony, not personal harmony thus they pursued a "way" believed to work for the benefit of everyone. The best and most natural sociopolitical system was that of the Western Chou dynasty as evidenced by its long-lived stability and social harmony. By clearly defining all words in the language so no ambiguities existed between people, by ordering those people in distinct hierarchies and by teaching them how to properly interact with each other, perfect social harmony could be obtained. Education and virtuous role models for the people to emulate insured that all played their prescribed roles in good form and that discord was eliminated. Society, thus, is the highest good because it takes disorderly and contentious humans and arranges them in a system of peace, stability, respect, virtue and social harmony as all strive to follow the prescribed "way."

3. What does it mean when a minority religion, such as Judaism or Islam, becomes "absorbed" by Chinese (or Indian) society?

Both the Chinese and Indian societies, with their vast throngs of people, tremendously rich and variegated culture and long history display the remarkable ability to "absorb" foreign religions or enclaves. China's greatness and wealth often attracted groups of merchants seeking profits, missionaries gathering converts, or ethnic groups fleeing persecution elsewhere. In periods of time when foreigners were welcomed, such as the T'ang or Sung dynasties, these groups of people would generally secure the blessing of the emperor to establish residence in China. With time, particularly since distances were great and traveling them very difficult, the people in these groups married local Chinese and bore children who then also married local Chinese and so on. After several generations, the foreignness of the original enclave often declined and with the scattering of enclave inhabitants, such as during the chaos accompanying war or strife, the original identity and culture would be lost.

Some settlements, such as the Jewish peoples of India or many of the Muslims of China, managed to carefully guard their culture and maintain it over generations. Others, such as the Jewish or Nestorian Christian peoples of China were completely "absorbed" having lost almost all notion of their heritage. They had essentially become "Chinese."

Questions For Class Discussion

1. What do you think of the concept of dharma?

2. Why is vegetarianism a natural offshoot of Hindu beliefs?
   When the Hindu belief of ahimsa, or nonviolence and reverence for all life, is applied to the everyday task of food preparation it is easy to understand why many pious Hindus are vegetarians.

3. Read the first three of Buddha's Four Noble Truths. Do these beliefs still have any relevance in the materialistic culture of our age?

4. Hinduism (as well as Indian culture in general) can be compared to a sponge in that both absorb much of what they come in contact with. Is this a fair analogy?
   Buddhism in India was eventually absorbed by Hinduism and disappeared. Also, many of the conquerors of India became completely Indianized. Indeed, as other religions came into India, such as Judaism and Islam, they were often forced to incorporate the caste system into their own organizations---thus making them resemble Hinduism as much as their original roots.

5. Discuss the following Confucian statement is valid "People must want to do right, and that can be achieved only by internalizing morality. When force or punishment have to be used, the social system has broken down"?

6. How do Confucian views of life and humanity's worth compare with those of Hinduism? With those of Christianity?
   Answers will vary. It might be noted, however, that Confucianism encourages "the enjoyment of living" and emphasizes life in this sphere. The Hindu search for moksha involves giving up everything in hopes of being reincarnated at a better stage in the next life. Christianity's view of original sin insured that Christians look to a place in heaven after this life.

7. What do you find (if anything) most appealing about Taoism? Why?

8. Using your understanding of Hinduism and Islam, list some reasons why the two religions have had difficulty at various times coexisting in India.

The Islamic belief of a jihad against nonbelievers and the Hindu taboo against killing cows, which contrasted with the Islamic taboo against eating pigs, combined to make life difficult between the two groups---especially among the more devout believers of both religions. Also, the Hindu characteristic of absorbing many cultures has tended to worry Muslims during periods of Hindu fundamentalism.

Multiple Choice Questions

1. Which of the following is <u>not</u> one of the sacred texts of Hinduism?
    a. The Vedas
    b. The Mahabharata
    c. The Bhagavad Gita
    d. The Upanishads

2. Which of the following is <u>not</u> a central doctrine in Hinduism?
    a. Karma
    b. Reincarnation
    c. Dharma
    d. Priesthood authority

3. Belief in reincarnation probably began with:
    a. Harappan civilization.
    b. Aryan civilization.
    c. Mauryran civilization.
    d. Kushan civilization.

4. The Hindus believe that good and evil:
    a. are separate forces forever in conflict.
    b. contained in all things, even the gods.
    c. contend for control of men's lives.
    d. are limited only to things of this world.

5. Zoroastrianism began in:
    a. India.
    b. China.
    c. Persia.
    d. Sri Lanka.

6. Zoroastrianism believes that good and evil:
    a. are two forces fighting for the control of the cosmos.
    b. do not exist.
    c. exist only in the minds of men.
    d. are really one force.

7. Buddhism was founded by:
    a. Siddartha.
    b. Shankara.
    c. Vishnu.
    d. Ramakrishna.

8. Buddhism became widely accepted and spread throughout Asia after the conversion of Emperor:
    a. Harasha.
    b. Chandragupta.
    c. Ashoka.
    d. Porus.

9. Which of the following cultures does not practice Theravada Buddhism?
    a. Laos
    b. Korea
    c. Burma
    d. Sri Lanka

10. Theravada Buddhism believes that salvation:
    a. is impossible.
    b. comes from ritual devotion.
    c. comes from good works.
    d. is a product of the Buddha's grace.

11. Mahayana Buddhism is generally found in:
    a. China and Korea.
    b. Tibet and Vietnam.
    c. Bali and Cambodia.
    d. Japan and Burma.

12. Zen is a Japanese sect of:
    a. Theravada Buddhism.
    b. Chavaka Hinduism.
    c. Vendanta.
    d. Mahayana Buddhism.

13. Confucianism provided the moral and social foundation of:
    a. Burma.
    b. India.
    c. China.
    d. Tibet.

14. The founder of Taoism was:
    a. Lao Tze
    b. Mencius
    c. Chuang tze
    d. Hsun-tzu

15. Which of the following countries does not have a significant Islamic population?
    a. Indonesia
    b. Malaysia
    c. India
    d. Japan

CHAPTER 5
Medieval India and Southeast Asia

Outline Of Main Ideas
Medieval India: the arts, trade, literature; misery in the north.

A. Early Islamic Influence in India
   - the Islamic invaders; views of Indians as infidels; the attraction of plunder and the establishment of Islam in north India
   - the spread of Islam to Southeast Asia; Southeast Asian culture before the influx of Indian and Chinese culture

B. The Islamic Advance into India
   - Central Asian Turks; Mahmud of Ghazni's plundering expeditions; the attraction of India; Rajput resistance; the spread of the Turco-Afghan empire in north India; the Delhi sultanate; the destruction of Bengal; north India's inability to coordinate a defense

C. The Delhi Sultanate
   - the status of the Hindus and jizya; the dhimmis; the gradual softening of Muslim rule; the Deccan and its Marathas; problems with internal power struggles and intrigue; Mameluke armies; general mistrust of the Islamic government; the fusion of Hindu and Iranian culture

i. Notable Sultans: Ala-Ud-Din Khalji
   - repulsion of the Mongol invaders; tight control over military force and society; the introduction of heavy agriculture taxes; economic control of surpluses; forays into the Deccan; the collapse of the Ala-ud-din system and resentment incurred against it

ii. The Tughluqs
   - the founder; Mohammed Tughluk; strict Islamic rules and conquest; Firuz Tughluq; a constructive administration; views towards the Hindus; the invasion of Tamerlane; fragmentation of the Delhi sultanate

iii. Sikander Lodi
   - Sikander and the further Indianization of Muslim rule; the rise of the bhakti religious movement and the sufis blossoming

D. South India
   - the south's semi-feudal system of rule; religious centers; flourishing trade and art; wealth and prosperity in the southern system

   i. Temple Builders and Rival Kingdoms
      - the age of faith; Ajanta and Ellora; free-standing temples; revenues and temple construction; the combination of religious and marketing centers

   ii. The Cholas
      - maritime trade and naval power; Ceylon; Chola expansion and decline; bronze and sculptural art; the problems of determining day-to-day culture

   iii. Vijayanagara: Empire of Victory
      - The Vijayanagara empire and its magnificent capital; views towards minorities; Krishna Deva Raya; destruction

E. The Eastward Spread of Islam
   - early merchants and their conversion to Islam; the spread of Islam to Malaya; Islam as a facilitator of trade; the spread of Islam to other parts of Southeast Asia and obstruction by the West; the adaptation of Islam to Southeast Asian culture

F. Non-Muslim Southeast Asia
   - Indian, Chinese, Malayan and Buddhist cultures in Southeast Asia; Burma (Myanmar) and Siam (Thailand) as mixtures of peoples

G. Medieval Burma and Thailand
   - the influx of Burmese and Thais from the north; minorities pushed into the highlands; Indian culture; agriculture; the Mons and the Pagan Kingdom; the Mongol invasion; the Toungoo dynasty; Buddhism; Toungoo expansionism; the Konbaung dynasty; expansion westward; British conquest
   - the Thai conquest of Angkor; the Mongol invasions and floods of refugees into Thailand; expansion into Khmer territory; defeat at the hands of the Burmese; the Chakri dynasty at Bangkok

H. Cambodia, Laos, and Vietnam
   - the Khmer people; the kingdom of Funan; Angkor Thom—the capital

   i. Angkor: City Of Monumental Splendor
      - King Yasovarman I; the city as a reflection of the Hindu cosmological universe; later Buddhist additions; the layout of the city; Angkor Wat; irrigation and hydraulic systems; collapse of the economic base and the city's lapse into ruin; the Laotians and their enemies

   ii. Vietnam: Expansion to the South
      - sinification of Vietnam on an elite level, distinctly Vietnamese culture on the popular level; resistance against northern expansionism; Vietnam's southward conquests; application of the Chinese government system

I. Malaya, Indonesia, and the Philippines
   - the wide-spread nature of Malayan culture but minor development of its political order; constant domination by outsiders
   - Indonesia's dominant island: Java; Sri Vijaya and its maritime trade; the Sailendra dynasty and Borobodur; the Mongols; Majapahit; the Islamic states
   - the Spanish in the Philippines; fragmentation and diversity; Islam and local animistic cults; the cultural impact of Spanish rule

Essay And Discussion Questions

1. What does the term "Indianization" or "Sinicization" refer to when used to describe government administrations headed by invaders or foreign powers?
   Indianization, or "sinicization" in the case of China, refers to the gradual adoption of Indian (or Chinese) culture, religion, and lifestyles by outside foreigners. Nomadic tribes invading from the steppes often found themselves in over their heads once the invading stopped and governing began. Indian civilization (and Chinese civilization) often proved to be much more sophisticated and complex than that of the invaders or foreigners. And, as a result, many nomadic conquerors quickly recognized the value in adopting Indian (or Chinese) culture in place of their own so they could govern without depending entirely on force. Similarly, some simply found Indian (or Chinese) art and culture attractive and enticing enough to cause them to abandon much of their own culture for something seen as better.

   In other cases, Indianization involved the utilization of Indian peoples or institutions in such a way as to create a hybrid sociopolitical system. Some foreign powers arriving in India brought with them an already sophisticated culture but welded to it portions of Indian civilization to produce a hybrid better suited to govern India. The Islamic invaders, for example, usually came with an already highly developed culture and religious system. Rather than abandon their Islamic heritage they adjusted their beliefs to accommodate an appreciation of Hindu culture and allow the incorporation of Hindus into their sociopolitical system. Thus, while the leadership retained its connection to Islam, it allowed Indian society to retain its connection to Hinduism so that all had a place in society.

2. By what different ways did Islam spread into South and Southeast Asia?

   Islam fanned out into South and Southeast Asia via many different routes. Islamic conquerors sometimes introduced the religion at sword point while destroying Hindu temples and places of worship of other religions, making Islam the dominant religion of the conquered area. Later, as the conquerors established control over society, many came to embrace Islam for its sophistication, doctrine and religious value while others accepted the new religion out of pure political prudence.

   In other cases, Islam spread along trade routes where Asians encountered it via Arab or Asian Muslim merchants. In these instances, as above, many converted through these contacts out of sincere commitment to the religion while others joined for the more practical reason of trying to lubricate relations with Islamic merchants. Islam also spread when Muslim merchants set up residence in Asian cities or established colonies along the trade routes where non-Muslims could encounter them.

3. How did distant nomadic invasions, such as the Mongol conquest of China, affect South or Southeast Asia?
In general, patterns of expansion and conquest began in the north and spread downwards, initiating shock waves that continued to impact peoples and civilizations even farther south. For example, the loser of a series of nomadic wars on the steppes of Mongolia might quit the steppes and push down through Central Asia before emerging in India to set up a new dynasty there—as in the case of the Kushan Empire in India.

Another scenario, as witnessed when the Jurchens invaded north China followed by the Mongol conquest of south China during the Sung Dynasty, huge numbers of dislocated Chinese migrated from north to south to flee the onslaught. The Jurchen invasion swept before it massive migrations to the Yangtse River Valleys of south China. Likewise, when the Mongols crossed into south China their armies pushed large numbers of Chinese into Southeast Asia, especially Burma and Thailand, where indigenous Thai and Burmese were then pushed into the mountains or other marginal regions.

Questions For Class Discussion

1. Is the analogy of the Indian "sponge" suitably applicable to the Delhi sultanate and its fate?

    Yes. Persian culture and religion did not overtake India but were absorbed by it.

2. Given the current problems between Muslims and Hindus in India, is a renaissance of the *bhakti* movement possible?

3. Was the great following of Mahatma Gandhi a modern day revival of *bhakti*?
Students with knowledge of modern India or a desire to know it are candidates for the last two questions. Both of these questions can and should be used in later chapters; both 15 and/or 19.

4. Compare Hindu and Confucian views of "this life" as opposed to "the next life."
Confucian thought asserted that humans have enough to do in trying to understand and manage human affairs without troubling about other matters. Indian Hindu writers, by contrast, felt day-to-day life was of "little consequence" relative to the next life.

5. Compare King Krishna Deva Rya's policies concerning minorities to those of Ala-Ud-Din Khalji. Which was more successful? Which of the two does your country most resemble?
Answers will vary. Although his reasoning is questionable by today's standards, King Krishna Deva Rya treated his minorities with "kindness and charity." Ala-Ud-Din, on the other hand, suppressed Hindus.

Multiple Choice Questions

1. Islamic culture was first introduced to early India from:
    a. Arabia.
    b. Persia.
    c. Baghdad.
    d. Afghanistan.

2. Indian influence in Southeast Asia dates from the time of:
    a. Ashoka.
    b. Buddha.
    c. Harsha.
    d. Porus.

3. India first encountered Islamic armies in the:
    a. 7th century.
    b. 8th century.
    c. 11th century.
    d. 12th century.

4. The first serious Islamic attack on India came when the Turks attacked repeatedly under the leadership of:
   a. Ali Pasha.
   b. Mahmud of Ghazni.
   c. Abu Bekr.
   d. Omar the Great.

5. By 1206 Islamic power was secure in Northern India and its base of power was transferred to:
   a. Bengal.
   b. Surat.
   c. Agra.
   d. Delhi.

6. The general policy of the Delhi Sultanate toward the native religions of India became:
   a. increasingly repressive.
   b. indecisive.
   c. increasingly tolerant.
   d. disinterested.

7. Mamelukes were:
   a. Turkish nobles.
   b. Court administrators and diplomats.
   c. Slaves raised to be professional soldiers.
   d. Islamic missionaries sent into South India.

8. Sultan Ala-ud-din Khalji:
   a. conquered all Southern India.
   b. defeated the Mongols.
   c. took Islam into Southeast Asia.
   d. forbade Islamic law in North India.

9. The Tughluqs were:
   a. the successors to the Ala-ud-din order.
   b. a Hindu resistance movement.
   c. Turkish revolutionaries.
   d. an Islamic religious order.

10. Chola power was based on all of the following *except*:
    a. its large army.
    b. control of maritime trade.
    c. control of the Deccan plateau.
    d. scientific advances.

11. The Vijayanagara Empire:
    a. was a great naval power.
    b. defended the Deccan against Islamic incursions.
    c. was a Buddhist state.
    d. was conquered by Sikander Lodi.

12. Islam spread from India to all the following states except:
    a. Malaya.
    b. the Philippines.
    c. Burma.
    d. Indonesia.

13. Which of the following Asian countries eventually succumbed to Mongol invasions?
    a. China
    b. India
    c. Indonesia
    d. Japan

CHAPTER 6
China and Korea: A Golden Age

Outline Of Main Ideas

A. Reunification of China
- the divided northern barbarian kingdoms and Buddhism; the Northern Wei; the southern dynasties; unification under the Sui dynasty; Sui Yang-ti

B. The Splendor of the T'ang
- T'ang poetry; reconquest of the empire by T'ang T'ai-tsung; development in the south; migrations of northerners southward
- the unrivaled grandeur of China; printing's dissemination to the West; inventions and commodities

   i. Ch'ang An in an Age of Imperial Splendor
   - the cosmopolitan and gigantic nature of the city; Ch'ang An's checkerboard layout; pastimes of the inhabitants; the arts; Buddhism; Ch'ang An's attractiveness to foreigners

C. Cultural Brilliance and Political Decay
- Hsuan-tsung and Yang Kuei-fei; Empress Wu; the Confucian revival and anti-Buddhism edicts; the An Lu-shan Rebellion; instability in the military; chaos

D. The Sung Achievement
   - China's glory; Sung China's barbarian policy: domestic development verses imperialist control of the steppes; Kaifeng and commercial development; the scholar officials; effective administration and flourishing culture; Su Shih

   i. Wang An-shih: Reform and Retreat
      - Wang's tax reforms; anti-Wang resentment; Wang's military and educational reform; the Khitan and Tangut barbarians

   ii. Barbarians in the North, Innovation in the South
      - the Jurchen invasion and the beginnings of the Southern Sung dynasty

E. The Southern Sung Period
   - sea routes and maritime trade; shipping technology; urbanization and Hangchow; urban culture

   i. Innovation and Technological Development
      - Chu Hsi; mechanized inventions; an industrial revolution?

F. The Mongol Conquest and the Yuan Dynasty
   - the Mongol threat; gun powder; Sung factionalism and General Yúeh Fei
   - the Mongol triumph; Kubilai Khan and his expansion south; Chinghis Khan: cavalry; toughness, terror tactics
   - sinification of the Mongols; Marco Polo

   i. Yuan China
      - China under Mongol rule; Chinese arts; Kubilai's brilliant administration; rebellion and the advent of the Ming dynasty

G. Chinese Culture and the Empire
   - the mature form of imperial China; the bureaucracy and gentry; the family; the dynastic cycle
   - China's culture; diet and cuisine; the rural landscape; transportation

H. Korea
   - the Siberian origins of the Korean people; Chinese influence; the Han occupation and Chinese culture; Korean independence

- i. Paekche, Silla, and Koguryo
  - selective adoption of the Chinese model of civilization; Korea's hereditary aristocracy; the rise and splendor of Silla; han'gul
  - Koryo; the Chinese model and Chinese art; civil war; the Mongol conquest
  - the Yi dynasty

- ii. Yi Korea
  - adoption of the Confucian system; the yangban elites; distinct Korean culture; printing; perfection of han'gul; bureaucratic factionalism; Hideyoshi's invasion; political decline and economic development

Essay And Discussion Questions

1. What developments in Southern Sung China resemble the Industrial Revolution of the West?

   The Southern Sung dynasty faced a geopolitical situation that differed greatly from that facing most northern-based dynasties of earlier or later periods. First, the tremendous migrations of northerners to the south and the relative short supply of developed arable land insured that the Sung would have to find other economics means to support the population. The answer lay in commercialization, urbanization and maritime trade with foreign countries.

   Relying on maritime trade for its revenues, the Southern Sung introduced new shipbuilding technology including greater utilization of the compass, multiple masts, separate watertight compartments, the sternpost rudder, etc. Technological development and new mechanized inventions in other areas such as agriculture, manufacturing and transportation also contributed to the general development of the period. Inventors and pragmatic proto-scientists introduced cultivation and threshing machines, spinning and weaving machines as well as channel locks, windlasses, and water-powered mills, to name but a few.

   All the while, markets for manufactured goods and new commodities spread throughout Asia driving individuals to seek new and better ways of mass production. Returns on economic ventures then produced the capital necessary for greater developments thus providing the Southern Sung with the steady streams of revenue that made it one of China's wealthiest dynasties.

2. What made the Mongols so formidable?
Coming from the steppes the Mongols possessed all the military vigor typical of most nomadic peoples. Skilled horsemen and hunters, the Mongols possessed tremendous stamina and speed that dazzled their opponents. They could cover seventy miles a day, or even one hundred and twenty miles a day if pressed. They required no supply lines, instead hunting and plundering as they rode. If they encountered no food they could always temporarily open the jugular vein of their horses' necks and consume the blood to sustain themselves. Expert marksmen, they generally rode up to a body of enemy troops, showered it with arrows and withdrew before the enemy could fully respond. This process proceeded until the ranks of the enemy were sufficiently broken and scattered, allowing the Mongols to charge through cutting everyone down in their path. In this way, the Mongols seldom had to actually face the brunt of the enemy's full strength.

The Mongols also used ferocious terror tactics. They generally spared cities that offered no resistance but often massacred all inhabitants of those that did. At the siege of Caffa, Mongols catapulted the corpses infected with the Black Plague into the stronghold in hopes of spreading the disease and weakening the defenders. The Mongols also spread word of their great strength through spies and informers spreading terror before them.

Another formidable characteristic of the Mongol armies was their flexibility and willingness to learn from the peoples they had already conquered. For example, only the utilization of northern Chinese and their various techniques of siege warfare allowed the Mongols to take the Southern Sung. And, the adoption of the Sung and Korean naval technology and tactics opened the way for the Mongol's attempted invasions of Japan and Java.

3. In what ways was the Korean (and Japanese) adoption of Confucianism "selective"?
Korea's proximity to China and the closeness of the two cultures insured that much of Chinese civilization eventually made its way into Korea where it was generally accepted and implemented. Chinese art, the form of government, Buddhism, and language (written only) all had an impact on Korean society and culture. Confucianism is no exception. However, like the nearby Japanese, the Koreans borrowed only those elements of Confucianism that suited their indigenous culture and social system.

China's examination system, for example, never succeeded in either Korea or Japan. Korea had long been ruled by an elite, hereditary aristocracy (*yangban*) which chafed at the idea of disrupting its dominance with a meritocratic system. The exam system offered to catapult previously non-elites into positions of power thus threatening hereditary privilege as the only legitimate right to power. Similarly, Korea's (as well as Japan's) elites maintained a professional military character that Chinese elites did not. Confucianism in China tended to denigrate the military in favor of a civil government which not only possessed more power but more status. In Korea and Japan, the military nature of the aristocracy became a part of their status and never received the same Confucian condemnation it did in China.

Questions For Class Discussion

1. What elements of the T'ang have distinguished it as "great" in the history of China?
   Flourishing T'ang poetry, art, theater, and T'ang China's cosmopolitan acceptance of foreigners and their religions are all indications of greatness.

2. The Mongols carved out the largest empire ever seen, the crown jewel of which was China. However they could not even hold it 100 years. Why?
   The harsh steppe culture of the Mongols taught them to become great warriors. Their martial strength and speed allowed them to establish the empire but did little to help them govern it. The failure of the Mongols lies in their inability to make the transition from conquerors to administrators. And, once removed from their steppes, they lost the martial edge that made them strong. Living in China made them soft and vulnerable.

3. Despite long periods of Chinese domination and heavy Chinese cultural influence, Koreans have maintained their own distinct culture. What are some examples?
   Hereditary elite, dress, diet (kimich'i), art, and language (spoken and han'gul).

Multiple Choice Questions

1. Four hundred years after the fall of the Han dynasty, China was reunited by the short lived:
   a. Sung dynasty.
   b. T'ang dynasty.
   c. Northern Wei dynasty.
   d. Sui dynasty.

2. When the Sui dynasty fell it was replaced by the:
   a. Ch'in dynasty.
   b. Eastern Han dynasty.
   c. Shang dynasty.
   d. T'ang dynasty.

3. The T'ang dynasty established its capital at:
   a. Anyang.
   b. Ch'ang An.
   c. Loyang.
   d. Nanking.

4. Which of the following figures was a major T'ang poet?
   a. Wu Chao
   b. Ou-Yang
   c. Liang Shou
   d. Li Po

5. The T'ang reconquered all of the former Han holdings except:
   a. Mongolia.
   b. Korea.
   c. Sinkiang.
   d. Northern Vietnam.

6. Probably the largest wholly planned city ever built was:
   a. Anyang.
   b. Nanking.
   c. Ch'ang An.
   d. Loyang.

7. Which of the following religions received official sanction in T'ang China?
   a. Buddhism
   b. Islam
   c. Confucianism
   d. Shinto

8. Su Shih was:
   a. the first Sung emperor.
   b. a Sung poet.
   c. the last Sung emperor.
   d. a Sung court administrator.

9. The Sung dynasty was finally destroyed in 1279 by:
   a. internal rebellion.
   b. dynastic struggles for succession.
   c. the Mongol conquest.
   d. famine and economic collapse.

10. The Southern Sung carried on trade with the rest of Asia by means of:
    a. maritime shipping networks.
    b. the Silk Road.
    c. the Great Southern Route.
    d. the Burma Road.

11. One Westerner who visited Hangchow shortly after the fall of the Southern Sung was:
    a. John Mandeville.
    b. Marco Polo.
    c. Peter Lollard.
    d. Henry Lawrence.

12. After conquering China the Mongols founded the:
    a. Manchu dynasty.
    b. Hong dynasty.
    c. Yuan dynasty.
    d. Hsia dynasty.

13. The leader of the Mongol invasion of China was:
    a. Chingis Khan.
    b. Hulanga Khan.
    c. Kubilai Khan.
    d. An'chou Khan.

14. Which of the following was not one of the three great states of ancient Korea?
    a. Paekche
    b. Annam
    c. Silla
    d. Koguryo

15. In the struggle between the states of ancient Korea the ultimate winner was:
    a. Annam.
    b. Paekche.
    c. Silla.
    d. Koguryo.

16. After being conquered by the Mongols, Korea eventually gained its freedom under the leadership of the:
    a. Choson dynasty.
    b. Silla dynasty.
    c. Yi dynasty.
    d. Koguryo dynasty.

17. The Yi government followed the pattern established by:
    a. Silla.
    b. the Mongols.
    c. T'ang China
    d. Japan.

18. Among the cultural achievements of the Yi was mastery of:
    a. Noh drama.
    b. printing.
    c. epic poetry.
    d. courtly dance.

CHAPTER 7
Early, Classical, and Medieval Japan

Outline Of Main Ideas
- Japan's geographical insularity and cultural identity; geography: the sea, soil, agricultural development; modern Japan
- the beginnings of Japanese society, Yayoi culture

A. Ties With Korea and Tomb Builders
   - late Yayoi culture and its connections to Korea; Chinese accounts of early Japan

   i. Mythical Histories
      - the Kojiki (Record of Ancient Matters); the Nihongi (History of Japan); the creation myths: Izanagi and Izanami, Amaterasu; Ninigi; the three imperial regalia; Jimmu and Yamato; Himiko the priestess; the Ainu minority and intermarriage; iron tools; continued early connections with Korea

   ii. The Uji
      - uji (tribal clans); the Yamato state and consolidation of the uji system; the religious and political role of leadership; Japanese animism and nature's kami (divine spirit); Shinto

B. The Link with China
   - the introduction of Buddhism from Korea; the adoption of the T'ang China model in Japan; Soga patronage and Prince Shotoku; the Seventeen Article Constitution and hierarchical status; embassies to China

C. Taika, Nara, and Heian
- rebellion and the rise of the Fujiwara clan; the pro-China Taika Reforms; implementation of the Chinese socio-political system; centralization; the move to Nara (710); Nara the city; the dominant role of Buddhism; the move to Heian (794); the divine nature of the Japanese emperor and his role in politics; court efforts to replicate T'ang China culture; hereditary aristocracy and rural administration; the expansion of state control; the general poverty of Japan and its barter economy; rejection of China's exam system and its meritocratic institutions

  i. Chinese and Buddhist Art
  - *the heavy influx of Buddhist art; the Japanization of styles; Horyuji; Todaiji*

  ii. Buddhism and Literacy
  - the impact of Buddhism on Japanese culture: cremation, vegetarianism; religious beliefs; Shinto and Buddhism; Buddhist sects: Shingon and Tendai; the adoption of China's writing system in Japan; the stimulation of education; the Kojiki, Nihongi and fudoki
  - the decline of the T'ang China model; reassertions of indigenous Japanese culture; the concentration of land in private estates

  iii. The Shoen System
  - the rise of shoen (private estates); court protection of shoen interests; dominance of the shoen and the decline of central authority; the failing political power of the emperor

D. Heian Culture
- economic and cultural development; the shoen and development of the outer regions; the application of the Chinese model to the outer regions; self-cultivation and refinement: clothing; the *Pillow Book*

  i. Murasaki Shikibu (Lady Murasaki)
  - background; talents and education; the *Tale of Genji*—a literary masterpiece

  ii. Art and Gardens
  - Japanese-styled art: painting, architecture; gardens as microcosms of the natural world; the connections between Japanese gardens and those of China

    iii. Kana and Monastic Armies
- the use of kana (phonetic symbols) and Chinese characters; Pure Land Buddhism; monastic and shoen armies and warfare; the rise of the samurai class

E. Pressures on the Environment
- population figures; the spread of cultivation; city building and demands for wood; deforestation; wood shortages and traditional Japanese architecture and homes; shipbuilding and sculpture; ecology

F. The Kamakura Period
- the Minamoto; samurai and feudalism; the shogun and feudal lords; the failed Mongol invasions; the decline of the Kamakura; Go-Daigo

G. Ashikaga Japan
- political weakness and the loss of central control; piracy; political unrest; a time of cultural blossoming: Zen Buddhism, architecture, painting, literature, the tea ceremony, Noh drama; civil war

Essay And Discussion Questions

1. Why did Chinese culture become so popular and accepted in Japan?
During the late 6th and early 7th centuries, Japanese society was a hodgepodge of uji clans united rather loosely under the rule of the Japanese emperor. Despite the high status of the emperor, however, he possessed no actual means for controlling Japan much beyond his own clan's territory nor did he possess any means to extend that authority. The Japanese did not even have a written language. With the introduction of Buddhism, however, Japanese began to recognize the greatness of mainland culture and its socio-political systems and institutions and to desire these for themselves. Not only did mainland culture appeal to the aesthetic senses of the Japanese, but it tempted Japan's leaders with the means to establish a powerful central government system that the Japanese had never known before.

Through the richness of Buddhist culture and its wide array of sacred texts, the Japanese began to learn China's language and adopt it as their own writing system using Japanese pronunciations. This in turn stimulated more interest in mainland culture until Prince Shotoku, the regent of the emperor, sent several embassies to

China to learn and bring back more useful items. The Chinese system of court rank, art and technology, architecture, concepts of central control and authority, the division of the country into prefectures, the writing system, and many other Chinese institutions were investigated and brought back to Japan. Using these systems and institutions, the court gained the ability to assert its own power and control while decreasing that of the uji clans in addition to enriching Japan's artistic and religious cultural realms as well.

2. What impact did Buddhism have on Japanese culture and lifestyles?
Buddhism transformed the landscape of Japanese culture by affecting not only the upper classes, but trickling down to the lower classes as well. Buddhism's introduction signaled the decline of the tomb-building culture and the beginnings of cremation in funerary rituals. Buddhist prohibitions of meat consumption caused most Japanese to become vegetarians (except for fish and an occasional bird). Buddhist images of afterlife and heavenly beings became commonplace along with the many Buddhist temples and monasteries. Buddhist monks came to be associated with death and conducted most funeral arrangements as well as being recognized as holy men with special powers over demons and monsters.

Among the elites, Buddhism offered a daily regime of meditation, sutra-reading, prayer and mantra-chanting. Among the peasants, Buddhist monks sometimes held lectures and offered hope of a better life to come alongside explanations as to why this life contained so much misery. Samurai often turned to Buddhism to bring solace to their disturbing livelihood while others abandoned their occupations to enter a monastery and concentrate on higher things.

Buddhism eventually came to have political power and incur the wrath of emperors and shoguns alike. Somehow, however, it did not replace Shinto, but forced Shinto to define itself and organize itself in such a manner that it could compete with Buddhism. Thus the Kojiki and Nihongi came into being. In short, Buddhism permeated virtually every level of existence in Japanese society.

3. How did the Japanese emperor differ from the Chinese emperor?
In some ways, Japan's emperor imitated the Chinese emperors, particularly since much of the Japanese government system was imported directly from China. One major difference, however, lies in the source of their right to reign. In China, Confucianism's dominant role in Chinese political culture insured that the ideal of "virtuous rule"

would always remain the basis for political legitimacy. In other words, in China, an emperor had the right to rule by virtue of his "virtue." And, as soon as that emperor lost this "virtue" he lost the right to rule from Heaven and the people could then legitimately toss he and the ruling clan out of power replacing them with a new dynasty. Thus, China has had several ruling clans or dynasties in the course of its history. These clans remained preeminent until removed from power by someone more powerful and thus more "virtuous" than themselves. After losing power, the ruling clan became no different from anyone else.

In Japan, the emperor's situation is quite different. Because he does not derive his right to rule from his own "virtue" or any other personal characteristic but claims it by right of birth, his legitimacy is infallible. Regardless of his station in life, he is always the "emperor" because he is the direct descendent of Amaterasu. The right to reign is lodged in the family line, not in how they act.

Access to power also differs. Because the Chinese emperor's power stems from his being able to maintain that power and convince other Chinese of his virtue, Chinese emperors generally ruled—that is they possessed power to act and formulate policy for China. Once ousted, however, the old emperor no longer held any significant claim to the throne. In Japan, however, emperors did not always rule. From the Kamakura period onward the military government of the shogun established policy, not the emperor and his bureaucracy. In fact sometimes the emperor was so poor he had to sell his calligraphy in order to pay his bills, and, during the Tokugawa period, the emperor did not even live in the capital. Nevertheless, despite his poverty and alienation from the corridors of power, the emperor continued to reign as such. The shogun himself paid token respect to the emperor even while completely disregarding his political wishes.

Questions For Class Discussion

1. What are some possible reasons for the preeminent role of nature in Shinto?
Japanese geography insures that nature assumed a dominant and powerful role that Japanese had to both contend with and work with. Agriculture in Japan is difficult due to its acidic, mountainous landscape. Numerous rivers carry away soil and carve up the landscape with ravines. The sea both protects and feeds Japan. These examples, plus, the many natural disasters which befall Japan make nature supremely important in Japanese life. Thus it is reasonable to assume that the early followers of Shinto would

look toward nature as a powerful controlling force that it was. Finally, the beauty of Japan's natural realm is stunning--capable of deeply moving just about anyone.

2. How did Prince Shotoku's *Seventeen Article Constitution* change Japan's sociopolitical system?
It promoted the supremacy of the ruler, centralized the government, assured reverence for Buddhism and patronage for Confucianism, and represented an attempt to replace Uji leaders with bureaucratic officials. Many of theses changes were based on the Chinese pattern.

3. Professor Murphey wrote that "to get a glimpse of what T'ang China was like, one must go to Japan." What does he mean?
Dr. Murphey's quote refers to the observation that the Japanese have better preserved the art, architecture and cultural elements of the T'ang dynasty than the Chinese themselves have. Such assertions could also be made in a limited sense about the fields of family structures and networks, government, and religion.

4. What do the writings of Murasaki Shikibu tell us about the lives of women in Heian Japan?
Not much is indicated about women outside the upper classes. For those of Murasaki's social status, women were well educated, free to write, played a more prominent role in family matters, and had more sexual freedom than women in later Japan.

5. What cultural and political changes introduced during the Ashikaga period had a long-lasting effect on Japanese history and civilization?
The flowering of culture, as seen in the growth of Zen Buddhism, the tea ceremony, Noh drama continue to affect Japan even today. Politically, the arrival of the West and the breakdown of central control left Japan's political arena filled with warlords all fighting to preserve their own power. Warlords and their culture then went on to dominate Japanese society until 1868.

Multiple Choice Questions

1. Which of the following is not one of the four major islands of Japan?
    a. Honshu
    b. Hokkaido
    c. Okinawa
    d. Kyushu

2. One of the native population groups of Japan were the:
    a. Ainu.
    b. Lung Shan.
    c. Hmong.
    d. Khmer.

3. Nara period Japan borrowed much of its culture from:
    a. Mongolia.
    b. T'ang China.
    c. Han China.
    d. the Yi of Korea.

4. The modern name for Heian is:
    a. Tokyo.
    b. Edo.
    c. Kyoto.
    d. Osaka.

5. The Shogun was the:
    a. title of the Japanese emperor.
    b. military leader of Japan.
    c. religious leader of Japan.
    d. highest ranking possible in Zen.

6. How many times did Japan successfully avoid being invaded by Mongol conquerors?
    a. On one occasion
    b. Twice
    c. Three times
    d. The Mongols never tried to invade Japan.

7. The Ashikaga Shogunate saw the full flowering of:
    a. nationalism.
    b. the Shinto Renaissance.
    c. Samurai culture.
    d. Korean influence.

8. Which of the following was not a distinctive aspect of Ashikage society?
    a. Noh drama
    b. The tea ceremony
    c. Zen Buddhism
    d. Taoism

9. Toyotomi Hideyoshi did all of the following except:
    a. Conquer most of Japan.
    b. disarm Japan's commoners.
    c. conquer Korea.
    d. re-establish rigid class patterns.

10. At the death of Hideyoshi:
    a. Japan was conquered by Korea.
    b. Genji became Shogun.
    c. Tokugawa became Shogun.
    d. Japan fell into a hundred years of civil war.

CHAPTER 8
Mughal India and Central Asia

Outline Of Main Ideas

A. The Mughals in India
    - discord in northern India; the Lodis

  i. Babur and the New Dynasty
     - Babur's background; the conquest of northern India; the Mughal dynasty proclaimed; visionary leadership and the infusion of Persian culture; Indian prosperity and development; Delhi and Agra; flourishing culture

  ii. Akbar's Achievement
  - Humayun; Akbar's succession and India culturization; Akbar's inclusive-style administration; expansion and empire-wide administration; reforms beneficial to Hindus; Akbar's gardens and his views towards religion

  iii. Akbar, the Man
  - brilliant yet illiterate; intelligent yet unpredictable; inventive; religious beliefs; luxury, Akbar's desire for an heir; the rebellion of his son and Akbar's death

  iv. Jahangir and Shah Jahan
     - court luxury at Agra; the Indianization of art and leadership; Shah Abbas and Iranian court intrigues
     - luxury under Shah Jahan; Taj Mahal; Delhi; Shah Jahan's imprisonment

v. The Reign of Aurangzeb: Repression and Revolt
   - Aurangzeb's ruthless and orthodox Muslim leadership; declining revenues and increasing taxes, revolts and banditry; the failed military campaigns to the south

vi. Sects and Rebels: Rajputs, Sikhs, and Marathas
   - the Rajputs and their defense of Hindu India; Sikhism and Guru Nanak; the Sikh military; Teg Bahadur; Guru Govind Singh; the Sikh Kingdom
   - the Marathas; their home base and militancy; Shivaji and Hindu-Muslim clashes; Tara Bai; feuding and administrative ineffectiveness; the Afghan invasion

vii. The Mughals and India
   - the decline of the tax-system; neglect of agricultural improvement; the strain of military expenditures on finances; luxurious court life; scientific backwardness; court neglect of the peasantry; Mughal collapse in the face of European and Chinese advances

B. Central Asia and Iran
   - China and India's problem of chronic invasion from Central Asia; the lack of historical sources; the steppes and deserts

   i. Nomadic Lifestyle
      - sound nomadic rejection of sedentary agrarian lifestyle; competing tribes; the harsh environment; the low population of the steppes; the importance of sheep and goat herds; the central role of the horse; the nomadic mounted archer-based military; the role of camels; nomad housing; fuel; handicrafts; diet; the tea trade

   ii. The Steppe and the Sown
      - the zone between agrarian and nomadic lifestyles; dependence and hostility between nomadic and sedentary peoples

   iii. Nomad Warriors
      - the lure of raiding; impressive nomadic mobility, weaponry and tactics; the absorption of nomadic culture into China and India

C. Iran
- the geography; the Persian empire, Cyrus and Darius I; Iranian-Indian relations; the Abbasid Caliphate, the Seljuks; the Mongols and Tamerlane; the Safavids; Shah Abbas the Great and Persian prosperity

Essay And Discussion Questions

1. How did the differing administrative styles and values of Akbar and Aurangzeb lead to radically different political results?

    Akbar viewed himself as a ruler of India first and a Mughal second. In other words, Akbar's reign focused on inclusive policies which accommodated a broad range of people by granting India's differing social groups a place within the administration and by promoting a tolerant society in which they could prosper. In return, these groups supported the regime. For example, he appointed Hindus to serve at court, employed them in his military and even married two so as to symbolically unify the diversity of India. As a result, many of the Hindu people lent their support to Akbar allowing him to establish effective control over the entire empire and set the stage for peace and prosperity for virtually everyone.

    Aurangzeb on the other hand took just the opposite approach. Rather than promoting unity despite diversity he sought to advocate Muslim orthodoxy and force all others to either conform to or submit to it. His harsh policies alienated Hindus and other non-Muslims to the point of rebellion. Such rebellions consumed revenues, both in taxes lost from rebel areas and in the military expenditures needed to suppress them. More importantly, however, such harshness sapped the credibility of the government. While Aurangzeb may have been a powerful leader, he was hated and set in motion the declineend of Mughal power in India.

2. What characteristics of the nomadic peoples made them "barbaric" to the civilizations of India and China?

    The primary difference between the nomadic peoples of the steppes and those of India or China lay in their basic lifestyles. Indian and Chinese society based itself on sedentary agriculture requiring stability, peace and mutual cooperation in order to function. The nomadic peoples, however, rejected what they saw as stifling and dull agrarian life for the freedom of the open steppes. Strength, independence and freedom were preferred over stability and mutual dependence.

To civilized Indians and Chinese the nomads were "barbaric" because they relied upon their martial strength for their survival. Nomads often raided Chinese or Indian settlements for necessary goods like iron or grains and fought each other for grazing rights. They generally did not have a written language, nor cities, and no particularly developed artistic tradition. And, to the disdain of Indians and Chinese with their rich philosophic and religious traditions, the nomad peoples worshipped animistic gods and held to shamanistic traditions. Nomads also dressed in animal skins and consumed large quantities of animal products to the chagrin of Buddhists who abhorred the slaughter of animals. In short, the lack of culture and signs of civilization, their reliance on their martial skills, and their willingness to attack and raid the communities of China and India with great slaughter made them absolutely barbaric to and greatly feared by the settled peoples.

3. What led to the decline of Mughal rule in India?
The Mughal decline can be linked to several developments, many of which have become standard explanations for the decline of dynasties in Asia. Extravagant court luxury and the construction of sumptuous palaces with its accompanying tax increases, alienation of the Hindu minority and their subsequent rebellions, and ill-advised military expeditions to the south all eroded the fiscal strength of the empire as well as divided political support for the regime.

In addition to these standard explanations, however, the Mughals failed to care for the source of their revenue. The tax system as established by Akbar became increasingly neglected by the court and soon benefitted the tax collectors more and more and the court less and less. Agriculture, on which the empire was based, received little attention at court. No one moved to further irrigation, introduce agricultural technology, or promote agricultural productivity and development. Thus, the living standards of the peasants declined while court life and luxury prospered. Industry and technology also languished under Mughal rule, allowing the Europeans to pass India's level of technological advancement for the first time. In essence, the court failed to protect and maintain the system that provided revenues just at a time when its consumption of taxes reached all time highs. Naturally, this weakened Mughal legitimacy and control and helped pave the way for their ouster.

Questions For Class Discussion

1. Why did many devout Muslims choose to withdraw their support for Akbar?

Many Muslims became enraged at his defiance of Islam's ban on the depiction of nature and his retraction of the special taxes on Hindus. Also, he married non-Muslims and generally refused to follow orthodox Islamic beliefs.

2. What elements of Akbar's administrative policies and philosophy allowed him to be successful? Which aspect of Akbar do you admire most?
Answers will vary. Issues to look for include: diplomacy, effective administration, his ruling as an Indian rather than as a foreign despot, his religious tolerance, etc.

3. Throughout history many minority leaders have ruled over a majority that was culturally distinct from themselves. What lessons might these minority leaders have learned, if any, from the example of Aurangzeb and his rule?
Imposing the strict views of a religious minority on a non-believing majority tends to generate resentment among the majority. Additionally, among other things, excessive military spending leads to higher taxes and thus a greater tax burden on the people. Together, these two factors prompted the majority population to rise up in revolt and overthrow Aurangzeb's regime.

4. What outside pressures lead the Sikhs to assume a strident military posture for their defense? What function does this militarism serve today?
Continuous attacks by Jahangir, Shah Jahan and Aurangzeb forced the Sikhs to fight or lose their homeland and religion. Today many Sikhs support having a homeland of their own (Kalistan). Even of the remainder who do not, most feel abused and/or betrayed by the Hindu dominated national government and thus find it necessary to protect their religious right via militarism.

5. What views/values might lead to the general nomadic conclusion that "all sedentary lifestyles are equivalent to slavery."

Multiple Choice Questions

1. The founder of the Mughal Empire was:
   a. Lodi.
   b. Akbar.
   c. Babur.
   d. Jahan.

2. Mughal culture came mainly from:
   a. China.
   b. Persia.
   c. Arabia.
   d. Central Asia.

3. The center of Mughal power was in:
   a. Hindustan.
   b. Punjab.
   c. Gujarat.
   d. Afghanistan.

4. Which of the following was not a characteristic feature of Mughal architecture?
   a. Walled forts
   b. Gardens
   c. Stupas
   d. Monumental buildings

5. Akbar's policy toward India's Hindus was one of:
   a. repression.
   b. indifference.
   c. toleration.
   d. forced conversion.

6. The Rajputs were:
   a. Akbar's most serious enemies.
   b. Hindu warriors from Gujarat.
   c. first enemies and then Akbar's trusted allies.
   d. Islamic fundamentalists.

7. Which of the following regions was *not* a part of Akbar's empire?
   a. Rajput
   b. Punjab
   c. Bengal
   d. Sri Lanka

8. Which was *not* a reform that Akbar introduced to India?
   a. He lowered taxes.
   b. He abolished forcible conversions.
   c. He made Sanskrit the official language of the Empire.
   d. He welcomed Hindus at court and in the government.

9. Akbar's attitude toward religion was:
   a. devoutly Islamic.
   b. atheistic.
   c. tolerant of all religions.
   d. Hindu by preference.

10. Akbar's successor was:
    a. Nur Jahan.
    b. Jahangir.
    c. Shah Jahan.
    d. Aurangzeb.

11. The emperor who had the Taj Mahal built was:
    a. Shah Jahan.
    b. Nur Jahan.
    c. Akbar.
    d. Jahangir.

12. The chief interest of Aurangzeb was:
    a. conquest and forced conversion.
    b. literature.
    c. Hindu theology.
    d. the building of cities.

13. Which of the following best characterizes Aurangzeb's personal religious beliefs?
    a. Islamic fundamentalism
    b. disinterest
    c. Hinduism
    d. tolerance of many religions

14. Which of the following groups did *not* stage a major revolt against the regime of Aurangzeb?
    a. The Sikhs
    b. The Rajputs
    c. The Mamelukes
    d. The Marathas

15. Maratha power reached its peak under:
    a. Govind Singh.
    b. Shivaji.
    c. Shah Abbas.
    d. Tara Bai.

16. Under Akbar, Hindus were:
    a. forced to convert to Islam.
    b. heavily taxed.
    c. given a major role in government.
    d. barred from the army.

17. The chief weapon of the nomads of Central Asia was the:
    a. sword.
    b. lance.
    c. composite bow.
    d. axe.

18. The Safavid Empire was founded by:
    a. Shah Abbas.
    b. Ismail.
    c. Tahmasp I.
    d. Darius.

19. The center of Safavid power was:
    a. Afghanistan.
    b. Northern Punjab.
    c. Persia.
    d. Anatolia.

CHAPTER 9
New Imperial Splendor in China
The Ming Dynasty

Outline Of Main Ideas

A. The Founding of the Ming
- general decline at the end of the Yuan dynasty; the White Lotus; the founding of the Ming dynasty and its brilliance

   i. Hung-Wu: The Rebel Emperor
   - Hung-wu's background and temperament; centralization and autocracy; grand secretaries and eunuchs; public beatings of officials; the expansive nature of the empire; Nanking the capital

B. The Ming Tributary System
- the attractive nature of Chinese civilization to foreigners; tribute missions and foreign trade; piracy

C. Ming Maritime Expeditions
- Cheng Ho's voyages; the economic element of the voyages; shipping technology; unprecedented scale but little impact; criticism and cessation of the voyages; the resurgent nomadic threat; Chinese disinterest in the rest of the world

D. Prosperity and Conservatism

- the locus of "civilization" and sino-centrism; conservative Confucian society; agricultural development and improvement; the effective Ming tax system and administration; commercial crops: silk

E. Commerce and Culture
- commercialization; the flow of silver and tax reform; merchant guilds and prosperity
- capital investment and commerce; proto-industrialization and technology; transportation networks; banking and capital transaction; "sprouts of capitalism" in the late Ming

  i. Patronage and Literature
   - the fine arts; Chinese painting; blue and white porcelain; technical compendiums; literature

  ii. Popular Culture
   - non-elite literature; performance art and other media of popular culture; opera; popular culture as a counter balance to elite culture; the values of the common people

  iii. Elite Culture and Traditionalism
   - China's focus on the past for guidance; Wang Yang-ming; the six maxims; the Grand Canal and inter-regional and foreign trade; the examination system; Confucian morality; the local gentry and self administration

  iv. Imperial Peking: Axis of the Ming World
   - the Ming move to Peking; selection of the new capital; the Great Wall; Peking's layout and orientation; structure in the Imperial and Forbidden Cities; nonstructure in the Outer City

F. Complacency and Decline
- growing problems; Westerners: Jesuits (Matteo Ricci, von Bell, Verbiest); administrative decline and eunuch power; fiscal decline and rising taxes; incompetent emperors; banditry and piracy
- Chang Chü-cheng's reforms and the Wan-li Emperor; the evil eunuch Wei and the Tung Lin Academy; court corruption and social chaos; the decline of Confucian morality; weakening military morale and technology

- the spread of rebel power under leaders Li and Chang

G. The Manchu Conquest
- the rise of the Manchus under Nurhachi; Manchu adoption of China's Confucian system; the Manchus as a rival power
- Wu San-kuei; the founding of the Ch'ing dynasty and the consolidation of power; the Manchus as preservers of the Confucian heritage

Essay And Discussion Questions

1. Ironically, while Europeans later fought wars over control of the sea routes in the Asian region, China abandoned its dominant position over the seas. Why did the Ming court decide to end the maritime voyages of Cheng-ho just as China reached domination of the Asian seas?

    The cessation of Cheng-ho's maritime voyages has several different facets, each of which influenced each other. The economic nature of the voyages proved to be rather unexciting to the Chinese. Despite the tremendous investment of time and revenues, the voyages produced little economic gain and were thus considered, financially at least, a major flop. Some exotic goods and animals made their way back to China, but nothing that could maintain any long term interest in the enterprise.

    Politically, one might argue that the voyages accomplished their intended objective: to bring all nations contacted under the Ming tributary system. Cheng's troops never sought total conquest, but instead tried to secure a stated declaration of loyalty to the Ming court and submission to its greatness. The Chinese accomplished this with considerable ceremony and display, thus, in a sense, nullifying any need to continue the voyages.

    Perhaps the most significant factor, however, involved the move of the capital to Peking from Nanking in the south, the resurgent nomadic threat in the north, and Emperor Yung Lo's constant attention to that particular problem. With the northern problems, Chinese attention turned away from southern maritime ventures to northern defensive postures. The maritime culture associated with south China had been tried and found uninteresting or significant. Perhaps this can be blamed on the fact that Cheng-ho's first and foremost objectives were political rather than economic (almost as if he was trying to accomplish northern-style political goals using southern-style economic means).

2. What is the difference and the relationship between Ming elite culture and Ming popular culture?

Elite culture pertains to the art, theater, literature and lifestyles associated with the wealthy and upper classes of China, particularly the court and the gentry. Popular culture refers to that associated with the peasants and lower classes of Chinese society. Elite culture has generally been defined by Confucianism and a commitment to Confucian values. Popular culture, on the other hand, was generally connected with Buddhism or Taoism and other folk-like religions. Nevertheless, the two sides borrowed extensively from each other.

While elite culture tends to reinforce the status quo, glorifying the status of those in power, popular culture tends to glorify those of either elite or common status who fight in support of justice, mercy and common good at the expense of the evil accumulation of wealth or selfish abuse of power. The poor maintained heroes who stood up for them and defended their interests. Ironically, these heroes could often be elites themselves, either peasants who had risen up via the exam system to elite status or a particularly concerned and benevolent judge, although many times they were outlaws or rebels.

Popular culture thus served as a counterbalance to elite culture by declaring the message that if the elites abused their power and authority they would not only face Heaven's wrath but peasant rebellion as well. It also provided a rich and colorful blanket of experiences in which China's commoners could find a meaningful identity and security.

3. What is meant by saying that the "sprouts of capitalism" can be found in the Ming dynasty?

The term "sprouts of capitalism" was coined by communist historians trying to track the progress of Chinese society through Marx's stages of development. Since China never passed through a truly capitalist phase as described by Marx, communist historians began to look back in history to see if China did indeed pass through something similar that might count as the same thing and thus justify the People's Republic's interest in socialism. The late Ming dynasty become one period that best fit this expectation and was declared to possess many "sprouts of capitalism" which emerged as a result of "proto-capitalism."

Such sprouts include the rapid commercialization of society, merchant guilds and the spread of markets, the heavy role of capital investment among these merchants, the spread of proto-industrialization and technology to various parts of China, the growth of transportation networks linking various economic centers, the rise of banking and transaction services that facilitated the movement of trade goods and investments, etc.

Questions For Class Discussion

1. What parallels (if any) can be drawn between the Ming maritime expeditions and the space programs of the United States and Europe?
Both are technological marvels that amazed their sponsors with the material and information they brought back. Both proved very expensive and produced little directly back into the economy. China's program was stopped due to budgetary constraints and new concerns of nomad activity in the north. Many assert that this loss of innovation and naval power lead to China being surpassed by Europe in technology on many fronts in just two short centuries. Some point to it as a harbinger of things to come.

2. What were the advantages of the examination system for bureaucratic selection?
One advantage was that more educated people worked in the government. Also, since some of the best career opportunities were to be had through education, more people became educated as they sought to gain a governmental post. Perhaps the most important element, however, involved the belief among the people that anyone with enough study and education could rise into the bureaucracy. Thus society had a vested interest in the government and participated in it.

3. Confucian doctrine claims that corporal punishment applies only to the ignorant masses. Is there any evidence that this concept survives in practice if not in theory in modern judicial systems?
Answers will vary. Look for discussion of police violence and abuses of power. More specifically, in punishment, both corporal and jail sentences, the "superior man" or those with status today, tends to receive lighter sentences for similar crimes.

4. If you were Cheng Ho what arguments would you make to continue the maritime expeditions?

5. What aspects of China in the late Ming astounded visitors from the West?
   The late Ming boasted substantial trade flows, immense resources (see quote by Ricci), major reconstruction efforts, high rice yields, efficient tax reforms (single lash), major urban centers with "factories," multiple technological innovations, bridges, boats, and a prosperous and thriving society.

Multiple Choice Questions

1. The Ming dynasty was founded by:
   a. Fung-lao.
   b. Hung-wu.
   c. Yung-lo.
   d. Cheng-ho.

2. The earliest capital of the Ming dynasty was at:
   a. Loyang.
   b. Ch'ang An.
   c. Nanking.
   d. Peking.

3. Which of the following was not an accomplishment of Hung-wu?
   a. He abolished the Imperial Secretariat.
   b. He broke the power of the court eunuchs.
   c. He conquered Korea.
   d. He defeated the Mongols.

4. Which of the following was not a Ming tributary state?
   a. Sri Lanka
   b. Korea
   c. Mughal India
   d. Japan

5. The Ming dynasty sent naval expeditions as far away as Africa (if not further. under the leadership of:
   a. Cheng-ho.
   b. Lo Pang.
   c. Yung-lo.
   d. Mo-tzu.
6. Which of the following areas was *not* visited by the Ming voyages?
   a. Java
   b. Arabia
   c. India
   d. Istanbul

7. Which of the following was *not* a feature of large Ming sea-going vessels?
   a. Water-tight compartments
   b. Use of the compass
   c. Iron bottoms
   d. The rudder

8. Which of the following was *not* a major Ming export item?
   a. Tea
   b. Sugar
   c. Porcelain
   d. Silk

9. Which of the following is a major works of Ming literature?
   a. *Tale of Genji*
   b. *Water Margins*
   c. *The Eight Trigrams*
   d. *The Good Earth*

10. Under the Ming the Grand Canal began at Hang chow and ended at:
    a. Nanking.
    b. Peking.
    c. Chang An.
    d. Loyang.

11. Toward the end of the Ming dynasty government fell under control of the:
    a. army.
    b. merchant class.
    c. nobility.
    d. court eunuchs.

12. The Ming dynasty was defeated by the:
    a. Mongols.
    b. Yi.
    c. Manchus.
    d. Yuan.

13. The founder the Manchu state was:
    a. Chang Chu-cheng.
    b. Wan-li.
    c. Lu Chi.
    d. Nurhachi.

CHAPTER 10
The Traditional and Early Modern Societies of Asia

Outline Of Main Ideas

- traditional Asia's group-oriented social system versus individualism; longevity and persistence of the system; the disadvantaged status of women and the young; the emphasis on having sons as opposed to daughters

A. Social Hierarchies
   - hierarchical status groups; education; the Southeast Asian exception

   i. Caste and Social Order in India
      - India's hereditary sociocultural system; development during a time of chaos to add order and security to society; jatis; the untouchables; the sadhu; "Sanskritization"; the caste as a source of identity and social ordering; the narrow geographic distribution and regional nature of jatis

   ii. Social Hierarchy in East Asia
      - the Chinese imperial (emperor) system; virtuous rule and paternalism in the government; the "state" family

   iii. Southeast Asia
      - greater equality of women; the "value" of daughters; bride prices; ownership of property; family names; sex; divorce; marriage; temporary marriages; women in politics

B. The Family
- hierarchical and group-oriented family systems; the elderly; family continuation and ancestor worship; the subjugated condition of women; the self-regulatory nature of Asian society; social mobility; the family as a welfare unit; the extended family

　i. Marriage
- arranged marriages; dowries and bride prices; the average ages of marriage; the status and responsibilities of women and girls; marriage and the advancement of family interests; divorce

　ii. Child Rearing
- pampering; public humility regarding children; discipline and male children; early childhood; dependency in adult males

C. The Status of Women
- the subordination of women; chastity and widowhood; footbinding; female infanticide; the lack of educational opportunities; concubinage
- women and power in the family; a woman's sphere of influence; the lifestyles of Asian women; the Southeast Asian exception; strong women; Muslim women

D. Sexual Customs
- elite culture; Japan's geisha; Chinese sing-song women; Tantric Buddhism; the Kamasutra; sex as ritual
- sex among the masses; fidelity before and after marriage; homosexuality

E. Education, Literacy, and the Printed Word
- education and power; the sacred nature of the written word; literacy and status; educated elites: Brahmans, gentry, merchants; literacy rates; paper and printing; literature

F. Material Welfare
- living standards; the family system; famine; drought; diet; tastes and cuisine; low life expectancy; disease; the inadequacy of ameliorating state measures

　i. Values

- humanity's subordination to the natural world; natural disasters as portents of heavenly displeasure; the nurturing role of nature
- the high value of leisure; festivals and entertainments

ii. Law, Crime and Punishment
- low levels of social deviance; personal guilt verse public shame; banditry and piracy; underworld crime; banditry as an indication of sociopolitical distress; secret societies
- laws and the court system; guilt on "confession"; torture and punishment; out of court settlements; justice

Essay And Discussion Questions

1. Most traditional Asian cultures had distinctly hierarchical social systems. What were the advantages of such a system?

The caste system of India developed during times of tremendous sociopolitical dislocation and discord. Castes, while generally criticized for their exclusiveness and/or their segmentation of Indian society, also possess a powerful inclusiveness which gives the system its strength. In other words, while caste laws can be said to form a barrier preventing unencumbered interaction with those in the caste, it could be equally stated that the caste regulations form a protective wall against outside abuse. Caste institutions serve as a mutual benefit society. Individuals within the same caste or *jati* band together, settle disputes as a group and work towards common interests. *Jatis* provide members with assistance in finding marriage partners and in securing other basic needs. The caste, in essence provides security beyond the family and allows individuals to maintain a common identity with a larger group.

In traditional Chinese society, the hierarchical system allowed for much more social mobility than in India. Educated individuals able to pass the entrance exam could rise to the highest class—the gentry—and eventually serve as officials in the government. Except for a few undesirables, such as barbers, prostitutes, and merchants, anyone could theoretically get an education in the classics and pass the exam even if the exam system realistically favored those with the time and money to get an education. Ostensibly, the process of study in the classics endowed one with the virtue and benevolence necessary to govern. Since, theoretically at least, China's system insured that the most virtuous governed, society enjoyed social harmony and stability as the result of their enlightened leadership. Meanwhile, these leaders taught the rest of the populace the proper roles associated with their social station, thus insuring the rest of society contributed to the general stability of society.

In Korean and Japanese society, the hierarchy did not develop into either a caste system or a fluid meritocracy but rather reflects something closer to the European experience. Elites ruled by nature of their birth. Individuals were kept in their place by their class designation and not allowed to engage in activities not prescribed to their class. The result, of course, was social stability. Social stability in this manner insured the dominance of the elites by keeping everyone else in their place.

2. What types of roles did the family play in East Asian society?

Individuals in traditional Asian societies were generally known by their family or clan and derived their self-identity from it. The family functioned as both a religious and social unit. In China, family gathering for the purpose of ancestor worship not only steeled family solidarity, but also connected individuals to a group that transcended the boundaries of this world. In India, various family units constituted the *jatis* which then combined with others to form the caste. While the caste and *jatis* form concentric rings of identity, the family lies at the center. Families also regulated themselves, often resolving disputes.

In China and Japan, family organizations or lineages could organize thousands of people throughout the various branches of a family and could regulate their behavior through family counsels headed by the chief patriarchs of each branch. Many of these lineage organizations actually planned strategies for the future like a corporation. On an individual level, unacceptable behavior could meet the sanction of these family heads, marriages could be arranged to enhance the prestige of the who clan, and children could have their lives planned out for them. In short, family heads often had tremendous power over the lives of individuals within the clan.

The family also served as a welfare unit. Sometimes great clans or extended family heads established orphanages or endowments to provide subsistence to widows within their family lines. If a poor family came upon hard times, it could always turn to a wealthier branch within the extended family for assistance.

3. How did the status of women differ in East or South Asia from that of women in Southeast Asia?

East Asian and South Asian women typically enjoyed less status than the men in their families. Buddhism's claim that women ranked lower on the hierarchy of beings than men augmented Confucianism's views that the proper role of women was subordinate to men. Possessing lower status, women had fewer opportunities for education, remarriage, property ownership and power within their own realm. The killing of undesired infant females, the upper class practices of *sati* and footbinding are all indications of the inferior status of women in East and South Asia.

Southeast Asians, however, failed to adopt these views towards women. There, matrilocal marriage, female control and inheritance of property and female dominance within the family stand in stark contrast to the patriarchal dominance found in both India and East Asia. In addition, the fact that children often possessed their mother's surname indicates distinctively different patterns of family structuring and reinforces the value of females to Southeast Asian families.

Questions For Class Discussion

1. What are some of the problems with a group-oriented social system? What are some of the advantages?
People with ideas outside the norm are ostracized. One result is that many new and innovative ideas are either never expressed or immediately rejected. Inclusion within the "group" may also involve conforming to superficial characteristics as well. For example, tall Japanese women sometimes have difficulty being accepted in society.

2. Which system—a group oriented social system as seen in Asia or an individualistic social system as found in the West—is "best"?
Of course there is no "best" unless "best" is arbitrarily defined, but this should lead to interesting class discussion.

3. What arguments might be made for continuing the system today? For abolishing it?

4. Professor Murphey asserts that Southeast Asian women took "an active and often initiating part in courtship and lovemaking." Discuss.

5. Why were young girls sometimes sold as servants or concubines? What did the family hope to gain?
   This question can be used for days of yore and/or current times. This question also lends itself well to role playing.

   Girls born to desperately poor families might have been left to die by the roadside, or killed. This practice can occasionally be found even today. If the girl had lived then she faced a very difficult childhood of physical labor with little to no formal education. When it came time for marriage the dowry inflicted much hardship on the entire family, in many cases the cost being as much as a year's wages. Compared to these two options, young girls sold into servitude or as concubines potentially enjoyed a much better fate. Girls sold to a wealthy family faced have less physical labor, recieved better nutrition and a had a slightly better marriage opportunities. Abusive relationships could and did exact a toll on these young women but many families considered it still a better option than abandoning a young female child.

   (With concerns to "child rearing," many of today's South Asian children are painted in black make-up, normally around the eyes like a mask, to show the gods the family has an ugly child in hopes the gods will leave it alone. [See p.199])]

6. Traditionally, Asians believed that nature was benevolent and not to be mastered. Does that view still hold today?
   This question is best as an assignment calling for some research of current events.

   Arguments can be found for both sides. Many of Asia's most populated cities are heavily polluted---Jakarta and Bangkok being prime examples. China's building of the Three Gorges Dam along with India's dam projects seek to "master" nature for human, not natural, productivity (electricity) on a massive scale. Some conservation movements are becoming larger and more influential through much of Asia. For example, Japan's recycling efforts have proved a huge success. The protest movements in India and even China against the aforementioned dam projects illustrate continued interest in preserving nature.

7. Should/could your country go back to the traditional Asian forms of punishment?
   Go over the options separately such as using guilt or shame, public executions, placards and labels, bodily mutilation, reeducation and reform.

Multiple Choice Questions

1. In traditional Asian societies, the means by which one could best improve one's social status was through:
   a. business investment.
   b. education.
   c. establishing a military career.
   d. state lobbying.

2. The pursuit of one's self interest in traditional Asian societies is:
   a. regarded with suspicion.
   b. held to be of great importance.
   c. placed above all else.
   d. considered to be a sign of wisdom.

3. Which of the following is an advantage that comes from having caste status in India?
   a. Aid was available from other caste members.
   b. Caste can give voice to individual needs of its members.
   c. Caste provides individuals with a secure social organization in which to live.
   d. All of the above

4. One way in which to escape the limitations of caste membership was through:
   a. marriage.
   b. education.
   c. religious devotion.
   d. economic advancement.

5. The caste system is an outgrowth of:
   a. Hinduism.
   b. Islam.
   c. Buddhism.
   d. Pre-Aryan society.

6. The role of women in Southeast Asian society:
   a. is highly restricted.
   b. is confined to the home.
   c. offers more opportunity than in any other part of Asia.
   d. is slightly more restricted than in Japan.

7. Prior to this century Asian brides tended to live:
   a. in the home of their in-laws.
   b. in their parents home.
   c. in their own homes.
   d. wherever they and their husband chose.

8. In most traditional Asian families:
   a. girls were given a good eduction.
   b. boys were spoiled and raised to be dependent on others.
   c. children were neglected until about the age of seven.
   d. all children were treated equally.

9. Until the late nineteenth century literacy in Asia was:
   a. confined to the upper class.
   b. higher than in the West.
   c. very low.
   d. about the same as in the West.

10. Traditionally, Asians tended to regard nature as:
    a. an enemy.
    b. something to be conquered.
    c. a force with which man must establish harmony.
    d. an entity of little importance.

CHAPTER 11
The West Arrives in Asia

Outline Of Main Ideas

A. Independent Development
   - the separation of Europe and Asia by Islamic civilization; Rome and Han China and the minimal contact between the two; the flow of gold out of Rome; Tang China and its lack of interest in or contact with the West

B. The Crusades: Europe Begins to Push Eastward
   - the commercial benefits of the crusades; the history of the crusades; cultural and technical borrowing from Islamic culture; the spread of commerce and economic development

C. Europe at the End of the Middle Ages
   - the backward state of Europe vis-a-vis Asia; socio-economic development

   i. Commercial Innovation and Expansion
      - the evolution of the workings of commerce; the use of trade and finance centers; the dominant position of Venice in the indirect Asian trade; Asian spices and commodities in Europe

   ii. Water-Borne Trade
      - Venetian wealth and merchants; Marco Polo and the splendor of Asia; the commercial advantages of Europe vis-a-vis Asia; geography; European curiosity of other civilizations; the discovery of sea routes to Asia

D. The Portuguese in Asia
   - Columbus; Portugal and the open seas; Portuguese ship-building and navigation; naval warfare

   i. Motives for Expansion
      - Western views of Muslims as the "enemy"; "Preston John"; Arabian control of trade; Henry the Navigator

   ii. Voyages of Exploration
      - Portuguese explorers; the influence of Marco Polo; early Portuguese contacts with India

   iii. The Portuguese Commercial Empire
      - the Portuguese in Goa; Portuguese military dominance at sea; Magellan; the colonies of Spain and Portugal

E. The Spanish in the Philippines
   - the flow of silver to Asia, New World crops; loose Spanish control in the Philippines; missionary work

F. Trading Bases in Asia
   - African bases along the sea routes to Asia; Europe's limited role in the spice trade; European traders working Asian markets; Europeans on the periphery; Portuguese and the rest of the commercial network along the sea lanes; the rise of Dutch and British influence and decline of Portuguese control; the legacy of Portugal

G. "Christians and Spices"
   - the Spanish and Portuguese missionary thrust; the slaughter of Asian "heathens"; Albuquerque; the Counter-Reformation in Europe and the Jesuits in Asia; the Canton trade

   i. Matteo Ricci: Missionary to the Ming Court
      - Ricci's background; an accomplished man of learning; his move north to Peking and acceptance at court; the adaptation of Ricci's message to China; Chinese interest in Western science and technology; controversy and expulsion; feedback and renewed Western interest in China

H. The Russian Advance in Asia
- Russian advances into Siberia; Chinese-Russian clashes; the Treaty of Nerchinsk (1689); Chinese disdain for the "sea barbarians" and high regard for the Russians

I. Japan's Christian Century
- Japanese curiosity and acceptance of Western things; inter-Christian contentions and governmental concern; persecution; the limits of foreign control; minimal European impact and success; European dominance at sea; the uncivilized nature of European sailors; Asian disinterest in Europe

J. The Dutch in Asia
- the Dutch challenge to Portuguese dominance in Asia; van Linschoten and Dutch expeditions to Asia; Dutch victories; Dutch interest in trade; The Dutch East India Company and its monopoly of the Asian trade; the Dutch Indies and Holland's sphere of influence; Coen in Batavia (Jakarta); harsh dealings with rivals and lawbreakers; the slow rise of Dutch administration; Dutch regulation and manipulation of production

K. The English in Asia
- English efforts to find a route to Asia; Fitch's account; The English East India Company; English interest in Asia; shipping technology; Shakespearean indications of European prejudice against Asians; royal support for the Company; the Midnall expedition; the Hawkins expedition; the Indian cotton trade
- harassment at the hands of the Dutch, Portuguese and Chinese; slow English progress; Will Adams in Japan; the Japanese trade

L. The English in India
- Thomas Best and the defeat of the Portuguese; Portuguese Jesuit intrigue against the English at court; Mughal cooperation; Roe and English interest in Bengal

Essay And Discussion Questions

1. What motivated the West's interest in Asia and what impact did that interest eventually have?

The proverbial "three g's" deserve mention in answer to this question: gold, God, and glory. Religious passions inspired the crusaders to initiate their quest to retake the Holy Lands. More to the point, the Jesuits and other missionary orders established proselytizing enterprises throughout Asia. In the Philippines, Spanish missionaries introduced Christianity, often at sword point, while elite-oriented missionary endeavors by Matteo Ricci and his brethren sought converts in China.

The lure of fortune to be made in the Asian spice, tea, silk or various other trades attracted not just the attention of merchants, but of entire Western nation governments. Europeans quickly discovered that whoever dominated the seas and their routes to Asia could monopolize that trade over the entire European market. Thus, despite their tenacious attempts to maintain their monopoly, the Portuguese lost control to the Dutch who in turn could not hold back the British.

Finally, national glory and honor came to be associated with the strength of one's position in Asia. Part of that glory came in the form of wealth derived from the Asian trade, and part from displays of the naval power required to maintain dominance on the high seas. The attractiveness of Asia and the above-mentioned benefits mentioned above led explorers, such as Columbus himself, to discover new lands and Europe's eventual colonization of most of the globe, either by claiming lands discovered while trying to get to Asia, building on lands enroute to Asia, or establishing footholds in Asia itself.

2. How did Westerners initially regard Asians and what impact did these perceptions have on Europe?
The few Westerners to visit Asia between about 1300 and 1700 found wealth, prosperity and civilization far beyond their wildest imaginations. Marco Polo's accounts of Yuan dynasty China astounded Europeans with tales of wealth and grandeur on inconceivable levels. Similarly, Portuguese visiting the "peacock throne" of Mughal India found immense power, luxury and affluence at court. Portuguese missionaries in Warring States Japan found the daimyo to be particularly well cultured and educated and the Japanese in general to be avid learners despite the rather advanced development of their own culture. Contemporary Jesuits in Ming China's Peking wrote home of China's great orderliness, highly developed culture and general prosperity.

With a few exceptions, such as the Mongols which left a bad impression on most Europeans, Westerners generally described Asia with glowing depictions and quickly began to bring many elements of Asian culture West. Tea drinking became widespread throughout Europe. Porcelains, silks, and lacquerwares could be found in the homes of many European aristocrats until the manufacturing technology spread to Europe allowing Westerners to make these items themselves. European philosophers found Asian philosophies enlightening, stimulating the humanists to argue, against the Church, that one could have an advanced civilization without any knowledge of God—like the Chinese. Even depictions of Chinese gardens, landscapes and people relaxing in their wealth were imitated and used on wall papers, cabinets, mantle pieces, harpsichords, etc. In short, Asian culture became the rage.

However, while some Europeans praised China, many condemned the Indians. Spanish and Portuguese explorers often brought priests with them who maintained little regard for the "heathen" Hindus or Muslims of India. On the contrary, those unwilling to abandon their religious views and adopt Catholicism were quickly put to the sword. Buddhists and Muslims in Southeast Asia met the same fate. Muslims faced particularly harsh treatment due to resentments harbored by the southern Europeans over the crusades and conflicts stemming from them. Unfortunately, these perceptions often led to brutal colonization practices and warfare.

3.) What factors gave certain European countries to ability to dominate the Asian trade and how did those factors shape the views of Asians towards the West?
As European nations discovered the wealth associated with Asia they began to compete for control of its trade. Unlike competition for trade today, which tends to revolve around board-room meetings and market strategies, competition then simply meant naval supremacy: whoever ruled the seas controlled the sea routes and thus the trade. As a result, Europeans fought many a battle over control of the sea lanes. And, often times these battles would be fought in the harbors or just off shore rather than on the high seas.

In some Asian countries, such as India and Japan, the use of military power awed and inspired the Asians. Recognizing the potential of Portuguese, Dutch and British vessels they struck deals with the Europeans in hopes of utilizing such power for their own purposes. The Chinese, on the other hand, had little interest in naval power and viewed it as little more than a confirmation that the Europeans and their warlike attitudes possessed more in common with the militaristic barbarians than with the civilized Chinese. Chinese viewed violence as the failure of more civilized diplomacy and viewed individuals who glorified in war with disdain.

Questions For Class Discussion

1. Starting with the Greeks, Europeans consistently looked eastward. Why didn't the Asians look westward?
Most often Europeans went East for reasons of trade as trade was an important aspect of their civilization. In general, wealth in Asia (excepting Island Southeast Asia) did not depend on trade to the extent that it did among Europeans. Most importantly, Asians (specifically Chinese and Indians) did not require anything from the Europe, whereas Europeans sought many commodities from Asia. See Part VI of Daniel J. Boorstin's *The Discoverers* for a good account of the Europeans' search for Asia.

2. Why was European penetration of Asia limited to the coastal areas of Asia?
The European nations most interested in Asia (Portugal, the Netherlands) did not have the military strength to defeat the native peoples. It would have taken a great land army such as that of France to defeat even a small region of India. More important perhaps is the question, why should the Europeans have sought to gain more control? The Europeans, in particular the government or private supporters of the expeditions, were mainly interested in spices which could be easily acquired from the coastal regions. There was no need to waste money on a military attack when fine profits could be made with the status quo.

3. Why did the Spanish and Portuguese feel compelled to inflict the cruelties they did upon the people of Asia? What did they hope to gain?
Most students will likely feel uncomfortable with this question. The students must remember that in the days before modern nationalism, killing for what you believed to be religiously correct was common. Translating this practice into modern terms may make it easier to understand: the wars, programs, and covert operations between the United States and the Soviet Union during the Cold War offer many parallels.

Multiple Choice Questions

1. Prior to the late fifteenth century European trade with Asia was monopolized by:
   a. Spain.
   b. Venice.
   c. Holland.
   d. Portugal.

2. Vasco de Gama:
   a. conquered India for Portugal.
   b. discovered Brazil.
   c. discovered a sea route to India.
   d. began Portuguese trade with China.

3. Prior to the Renaissance the major impediments to European trade with Asia were:
   a. the Arabs and Turks.
   b. long and hazardous distances.
   c. mountain ranges and deserts.
   d. all of the above.

4. The Han dynasty in China coincided with what period of European history?
   a. The Byzantine Empire
   b. The Middle Ages
   c. The Hellenistic Period
   d. The Roman Empire

5. The driving force behind Portuguese expansion and exploration was:
   a. Philip the Fair.
   b. Sebastian the Bold.
   c. Henry the Navigator.
   d. Alphonso the Wise.

6. The chief center of Portuguese trade with India was:
   a. Calicut.
   b. Agra.
   c. Goa.
   d. Surat.

7. The chief product of the Portuguese Indian trade was:
   a. silver.
   b. spices.
   c. fine gems.
   d. silk.

8. Which of the following was not a Portuguese trading center?
   a. Manila
   b. Goa
   c. Macao
   d. Malacca

9. The first missionary to successfully be accepted by the Chinese Ming court was the Jesuit:
   a. Matteo Ricci.
   b. Ignatius Loyola.
   c. Francis Xavier.
   d. Siguenze y Gongora.

10. The Jesuits tended to:
    a. preach to the Chinese masses.
    b. advocate the westernization of China.
    c. work with the Chinese elites.
    d. openly preach Christianity throughout China.

11. Spanish trade with China was carried on through:
    a. Hong Kong.
    b. Canton.
    c. Macao.
    d. the Philippines.

12. The chief product that China received from the Spanish empire was:
    a. sugar.
    b. guns.
    c. silver.
    d. jewels.

13. The land rival that caused the Chinese the most concern was:
    a. India.
    b. England.
    c. Vietnam.
    d. Russia.

14. The chief item that China received in its trade with Russia was:
    a. silver.
    b. furs.
    c. guns.
    d. timber.

15. In order to penetrate China the Jesuits:
    a. created rebellions throughout China.
    b. formed alliance with disaffected Chinese merchants.
    c. adopted Chinese language and culture.
    d. used military force to compel Chinese acceptance.

16. After 1640, Christianity in Japan:
    a. flourished.
    b. was suppressed.
    c. was confined to the trading ports.
    d. became the state religion.

17. Dutch trade in Asia centered upon:
    a. India.
    b. China.
    c. Java and Indonesia.
    d. the Philippines.

18. The chief vehicle for Dutch trade in Asia was the:
    a. Batavia Company.
    b. Dutch Spice Company.
    c. Southeast Asian Trading Company.
    d. Dutch East India Company.

19. The founder of the Portuguese Empire in Asia was:
    a. Vasco de Gama.
    b. Henry the Navigator.
    c. the Duke of Albuquerque.
    d. Bartholomeu Diaz.

20. The creator of the Dutch trading Empire in Southeast Asia was:
    a. Felix Cabal.
    b. Jan Pieterzoon Coen.
    c. Jan Huyghen van Linschoten.
    d. Pieter Gynt.

21. The first Englishman to circumnavigate the world was:
    a. Francis Drake.
    b. John Cavendish.
    c. William Hawkins.
    d. Thomas Coventanry.

22. The chief vehicle for English trade with Asia was the British East India Company. It was chartered by:
    a. James I.
    b. Charles I.
    c. Elizabeth I.
    d. Henry VIII.

25. Early English trade with Mughal India was blocked by the influence of the:
    a. Moslem clergy.
    b. Portuguese Jesuits.
    c. Dutch
    d. Spanish

97

CHAPTER 12
Manchu China and Tokugawa Japan

Outline Of Main Ideas
- China: greatness under the Manchus; the Ch'ing dynasty's rise and fall
- Japan: unification and prosperity; the Tokugawa shogunate's rise and fall

A. China Under the Manchus
   - the defeat of the Ming loyalists; Chinese collaboration and the Manchu minority; Manchu adoption of Chinese culture and institutions; the emperor and the bureaucracy; communications; admiring European accounts of China

B. Prosperity and Population Increases
   - the general prosperity of Chinese society; agricultural development and China's rising population; Chinese merchants and commerce; the introduction of New World crops; rice production; population figures

   i. Kang Hsi and Ch'ien Lung
      - Kang Hsi: patron of culture; relations with Jesuit missionaries; patron of learning; capable administrator; military conquests; the issue of the "sea barbarians"
      - Ch'ien Lung: patron of learning; patron of the arts; military campaigns; the emperor in his later years; Ho Shen; the decline of effective administration; the White Lotus Rebellion; corruption in Chinese society

ii. The Later Ch'ing: Decline and Inertia
   - the high point of art and literature; the decline in availability of official posts; frustrated examination candidates; the decline of official/population ratios; population growth surpasses production; rebellions

iii. New Barbarian Pressures
   - Chinese containment of Westerners at Canton; James Flint; the Macartney Mission; Chinese self-sufficiency and Western hopes for open trade; Western admiration of China; Western frustration

iv. Ch'ing Glory and Technological Backwardness
   - successes: bureaucratic competence; flourishing art and urban culture; prosperous society
   - problems: rural poverty; Chinese cultural arrogance; technological backwardness; Chinese merchant wealth and capital accumulation; Confucian attitudes towards science; rising population; militant Western powers; spreading corruption; banditry; rebellion

C. The Opium War
   - the reversal of the flow of silver (now a net drain on China); the rise of the opium market—a Chinese social problem; British and Chinese demands; Lin Tse-hsu; the Opium War; utter Chinese defeat; the Treaty of Nanking

D. Reunification and the Tokugawa Shogunate in Japan
   - limited Ashikaga control; warring clans; Japan's relative backwardness but extensive foreign trade; independent daimyo dominating a feudal system

   i. The Era of the Warlords
      - Oda Nobunaga; Hideyoshi; Tokugawa Ieyasu; measures of stabilization

   ii. Tokugawa Rule
      - the strong central government; government control over the daimyo, samurai, merchants and peasants; the Tokugawa socio-political order; dominance of the samurai class; the government monopoly of weaponry; Confucian values

    iii. The Expulsion of Foreigners
- Westerners and trade; the governmental ban on Christianity and persecution of Christians; isolation and Nagasaki trade

    iv. Culture and Nationalism
- advents of change: the rise of the merchant class, the dominance of merchant culture, "Dutch Learning," the Shinto revival

    v. Edo and the "Floating World"
- the growth of Edo and decline of the daimyo; Edo's population; the pleasure quarters; the heavy use of wood construction; cultural vigor

    vi. Hokusai, Master Artist
- Hokusai's background; the popularity of Japanese art in the West; the widespread influence of Hokusai's style

E. Foreign Pressures for Change
- the impact of the West on Japan; Americans in Japan—Perry's forced opening of Japan; Western-dominated treaty ports and Japanese nationalistic resistance; the imperiled shogunate in the middle; the Meiji Restoration

Essay And Discussion Questions

1. Why did the Ch'ing Dynasty court prefer to contain and limit Western trade, by restricting it to Canton, rather than open free trade like the Westerners wanted?

By the time European traders reached the shores of China, the Ch'ing court had already invested tremendous amounts of energy and resources to insure that nothing would come along and upset the status quo. Confucianism, with its exam system, restrictions on Chinese merchants and the military, emphasis on loyalty, condescending views towards science, etc., all served to prevent other social groups from obtaining power that could be used to challenge that of the Confucian scholars. The Chinese knew that foreign trade produced wealth. But they also knew it produced it for groups that generally served their own interests rather than those of the court or for "the good of all under Heaven."

From this perspective then, Confucian Chinese chose to grant limited trade, via Canton, to the "sea barbarians" to make them happy while maintaining tight control over it at the same time to prevent social change from disrupting Chinese society. Westerners also impressed the Chinese as an unruly, wild lot with too much body hair, lots of repugnant weapons and rather uncouth behavior. Ideologically, Confucian Chinese already considered all merchants to possess a lower order of morality because they pursue profit rather than cultivate righteousness or inner morality. Thus, the morally-deficient "sea barbarians" were viewed as nothing but trouble.

Also, China's economy before the Opium War was largely self-sufficient. European woolens and furs drew little attention from Chinese in general. Thus, the Manchu court felt no need to pursue open trade relations.

2. How did Ch'ing China's socio-political system differ from that of Tokugawa Japan?
Political power in Ch'ing China resided in the hands of the Confucian scholars. These men (women were not allowed to participate in the exams) studied the Confucian classics for years, passed the Confucian examinations, and were thereupon granted tremendous status and political power for their efforts. In short, the Chinese had a meritocratic (status based on merit) system. In Tokugawa Japan, the ruling class consisted of hereditary warrior elites: the samurai class. Status depended upon one's family and its connections with other elites. And, since the Tokugawa Period boasted a long, consistent peace, with very few wars or contentions, samurai status did not even depend on their military prowess as in times of old. Their power simply rested on their family connections.

China had an emperor who ruled the empire via an elaborate bureaucracy. In Japan, the ruler was a military officer or shogun who supposedly ruled under the emperor but actually ruled "for him". China's emperor held tremendous power while Japan's maintained virtually none. Their respective government systems also differed. Ch'ing China was a unified political unit divided into provinces and counties but administered by one centralized bureaucracy whose power extended down to the county level. Tokugawa Japan on the other hand consisted of numerous small domains (or *han*) each of which had its own laws, administrative bureaucracy and hereditary warlord overlord (or *daimyo*). The domains remained independent of the shogun who dominated them in a sort of centralized feudal system.

Also, the role of the merchant in Ch'ing China remained quite limited. Even after the Opium War, merchants and their wealth could only wield political power or influence if they could get support from someone with an examination degree. In Tokugawa Japan, however, the merchants of Edo and Osaka began to dominate Japanese society in their own right. Commerce brought immense wealth which gave Japanese merchants high status not afforded their Chinese contemporaries.

3. What indigenous factors helped the Japanese respond so quickly to the Western threat and what indigenous factors prevented the Chinese from doing likewise?

The Japanese were fortunate to be further east than China and rather uninteresting to Westerners vis-a-vis the Asian mainland. As a result, the Japanese had front row seats for the events taking place there and knew what was in store for them if they tried to resist as the Chinese had done. Many also point to the Japanese samurai class and its emphasis on "action" as opposed to "morality" which the scholars of China tended to prefer. Japan had also had extensive experience in borrowing culture and socio-political models from more advanced civilizations abroad, giving them a quick eye to recognize the value of new systems, technology or institutions even if of foreign origin. The Chinese, on the other hand, were much more accustomed to "barbarians" borrowing from them. Quickly assessing that the "sea barbarians" possessed little morality, the Chinese dismissed all Western culture as unfit for Chinese consumption. Similarly, the greatest triumphs of Western culture came in the area of science, which the Ch'ing Chinese had little interest in.

Also, the Chinese Confucian system had worked for some two thousand years and under the Ch'ing had only just reached its apex. As a result, the Chinese had little incentive to try and incorporate into it the novel trinkets or "monkey tricks" offered by the Westerners. The Japanese, on the other hand, were struggling to keep the Tokugawa system afloat. Samurai poverty and weakness in the face of merchant prosperity threatened the entire system. Something new, even if from the West, was a welcome sight to many.

Questions For Class Discussion

1. According to the author, Voltaire and other Enlightenment thinkers believed that "China seemed close to the Platonic ideal—a state ruled by philosopher-kings." In

what ways did the Chinese government reflect this ideal? In what ways did it fall short?

As the author states, the leaders of the Enlightenment admired China's emphasis on morality and education as the defining feature of government rather than hereditary succession as Europe then employed. What is missing from this vision, however, is that this system did not reach to the top; the position of the Emperor continued to be a hereditary title. While the Emperor-in-waiting may indeed have been well schooled, since he had no competition for the job he may not have been the best candidate. The bureaucracy could pressure him to act in a moral and righteous manner using persuasion and subtle threats of failure. But if adamant, the emperor could continue to do as he wished by surrounding himself with sycophants.

2. What is the function of nepotism and "corruption" in China and other Asian nations?
Answers will vary. Those against nepotism will mention unfairness along with the under-utilization of talent without connections. Those for it will discuss the strength of the Chinese patron-client networks and family structures.

3. Was opium use by the "self-indulgent upper classes—[along with] the disadvantaged" in China a cause or an effect of a declining dynasty?

4. To what degree are the nations that supplied opium to China to blame for the ills of the opium trade?
The author wrote, that this was a "Chinese problem." The traders were simply fulfilling a demand. However, the morality of such an assertion can be debated back and forth, depending on how one defines "morality".

5. How were the Manchu (1644-1911) and Mughal (1526-1707) regimes, both of foreign origin, able to dominate lands much larger than their own for great lengths of time?
Both conquer dynasties in the throes of central collapse (Delhi Sultanate, Ming Dynasty). Both came from outer regions not far from the old capital (Afghanistan, Manchuria). Both had great early leaders that successfully consolidated power and ushered in a period of cultural flourishing (Babur and Akbar, Kang Hsi and Ch'ien Hung). Most likely the most effective trait was the way both dealt with the indigenous cultures. While the Manchus did eradicate the "excesses" of late Ming culture, they remained firmly rooted in the scope of Confucian culture and indeed portrayed themselves as restorers of China's traditional greatness.

A modern day example of why not to ignore the examples of the Mughals and the Manchus would be Hitler's attempt to conquer and rule Europe. His disregard for the Slavs, Czechs, and other East Europeans became a major problem resulting in heavy expenditures of men and material trying to keep these people in place and under control.

Multiple Choice Questions

1. The Manchu Ch'ing dynasty differed from that of the Mongol Yuan in that the:
    a. Manchu armies were larger and more terrifying.
    b. Mongols tried hard to adapt themselves to Chinese ways.
    c. Manchus better adapted to Chinese civilization than the Mongols.
    d. Manchus enjoyed the support of Russia.

2. Which of the following was *not* a Ch'ing achievement?
    a. The creation of a new Chinese law code
    b. Expansion of the Chinese postal system
    c. The conquest of Japan
    d. Expansion of China's agriculture

3. Which of the following was not an achievement of the regime of Kang Hsi?
    a. Creation of a dictionary of the Chinese language
    b. Conquest of Taiwan
    c. Conquest of Mongolia and Tibet
    d. Signing the Treaty of Nerchinsk with Russia

4. Until the nineteenth century the only Chinese port Europeans were allowed to trade from was:
    a. Nanking.
    b. Hangchow.
    c. Canton.
    d. Shanghai.

5. Which of the following novels was written during the Ch'ing dynasty?
   a. *The Tale of Genji*
   b. *Dream of the Red Chamber*
   c. *Water Margins*
   d. *The Golden Lotus*

6. Which of the following was *not* a source of opium for the British opium trade with China?
   a. India
   b. Iran
   c. Vietnam
   d. Turkey

7. As a result of the Opium War, China was forced to sign the Treaty of:
   a. Canton.
   b. Nanking.
   c. Hong Kong.
   d. Peking.

8. The chief cause for the fall of the Ashikaga Shogunate was:
   a. peasant revolt.
   b. civil war.
   c. revolt among the feudal nobility.
   d. religious conflict.

9. The city of Edo is now known as:
   a. Kyoto.
   b. Osaka.
   c. Hiroshima.
   d. Tokyo.

10. The founder of the Tokugawa Shogunate was:
    a. Toyotomi Hideyoshi.
    b. Hokusai Sato.
    c. Tokugawa Ieyasu.
    d. Oda Nobunaga.

11. The center of Tokugawa power was in:
    a. Osaka.
    b. Edo.
    c. Kobe.
    d. Kyoto.

12. One of the main reasons that foreigners were expelled from Japan during the Tokugawa Shogunate was:
    a. they were pirates.
    b. missionaries were attacked by Japanese peasants.
    c. the irritation caused by arguments among rival missionary groups.
    d. foreign traders tried to kidnap the Emperor.

CHAPTER 13
The Rise of British Power in India

Outline Of Main Ideas
- • the collapse of the Mughal regime and disunity; rule of the English East India Co.

A The Mughal Collapse
- Aurangzeb and his weak successors; fragmentation and disunity in the Mughal empire; Maratha raiders and their failure to succeed the Mughals; internal discord; external Persian incursions; regional divisions

B. Westerners in India
- early European contacts with India; Western trade interests and Indian political interests; Portuguese then Dutch and British dominance; the distribution of Dutch and Portuguese interests in India

C. The Early English Presence
• early British efforts blocked by Portugal; ventures of the English East India Co.; English naval supremacy over the Portuguese; weak attraction of British commodities in India; powerful attraction of British naval power

  i. Territorial Bases
  - well-positioned mercantile bases and fortresses: Madras (in the south), Calcutta (in the east), Bombay (in the west); 1714 embassy and English attainment of the right to local administration

  ii. The Mughal and Post-Mughal Contexts
  - the decline of the Mughal order and the attraction of secure refuge within Company jurisdiction; merchant attraction to English stability and order; Indian

cottons; Indian prosperity and limitations under English rule; commercialization and collaboration

D. Anglo-French Rivalry and the Conquest of Bengal
    - Anglo-French competition and the French defeat; superior European military power; the "Black Hole of Calcutta" and the Battle of Plassey; English control of Bengal; Indian collaboration

    i. Robert Clive And The Beginnings Of British India
        - the background of Robert Clive; adventures against the French; victory at Plassey; Bengal administration; suicide

    ii. The Establishment of British Rule
        - British plunder and extortion in Bengal; defeat of the Marathas by the Afghans; the Board of Control for India; defeat of the Indian Bengal regime

    iii. From Trading Company to Government
        - indirect British administration via the Indian princes; Napoleonic wars and the seizure of French territory; the seizure of Maratha territory; Warren Hastings; Cornwallis; Wellesley; territorial expansion: the central Ganges Valley, Ceylon—tea and rubber in Ceylon

    iv. The Reasons for British Hegemony
        - Indian collaboration; British rule preferred to any Indian alternative; British efforts at honest, humane and effective government

E. The Orientalists and the Bengal Renaissance
    - British and Indian cross-cultural appreciation; Sir William Jones; British scholars of Indology; Ram Mohun Roy; the Hindu Renaissance; Derozio and Dwarkanath Tagore; the emergence of a Westernized India middle class; Rabindranath Tagore

    i. Calcutta, Colonial Capital
        - east India's hot, humid climate and "The City of Dreadful Night"; diseases; a major trade center and transportation hub; an industrial center; conspicuous wealth alongside slums

F. From Tolerance to Arrogance
- indirect British rule; some Indians thrive, some are ruined under the British system; very limited social or cultural repression; the rise of the Indian middle class; industrialization
- the British "need" to "civilize" India; the imposition and promotion of British culture; railroads, postage and telegraphs; British defeat at the hands of the Afghans; British defeat of the Sikhs in Punjab and Kashmir

G. The Revolt of 1857
- the British annexation of the independent central Indian states; angry Indian aristocracy and troops; the rebel capture of Delhi; the new view of Britain as an occupying power; British atrocities; no chance for an equal partnership between England and India

H. The Consolidation of the British Empire in India
- when were the beginnings of empire?; English East India Company interests; territorial acquisitions; Orientalist verses utilitarians philosophies regarding India; utilitarian victory and the move to "civilize" India; British education and legal systems in India
- Indian intellectual mastery of British and Indian culture; the rise of Indian nationalism; Western values and Indian yearnings for them (freedom, sovereignty, liberty, etc.); the unification of India via rail, telegraph, the English language, the press
- assessments of early British administration; the rise of an Indian identity; the exclusive nature of British culture; the backwardness of the princely states; backward rebels and educated Indian elites both demand independence

Essay And Discussion Questions

1) What circumstances served British efforts to establish a hold in and eventual dominion over India?
Mughal support, to the point of granting local administrative control or at least to the point of not ousting the British outright, allowed the British to get a foot-hold in India. British naval supremacy over the Portuguese attracted the attention of the Mughal court which sought British naval protection in exchange for certain privileges.

The decline of the Mughals and the "peacock throne" as a viable political regime in India and the failure of the Marathas to replace them meant the British had no true contenders for power in India (excepting perhaps the French). With no other power in India to act as an alternative, the British were free to construct whatever system best suited them. Fortunately for the British, the old Indian habit of ruling through local princes, as the Mughals had done, allowed the colonialists to take power gradually since they could not have ruled the entire subcontinent outright without first building a power base.

From the Indian perspective, many were more than happy to work under British rule which provided a relatively safe haven and opportunities for advancement not found anywhere else. Thus, those Indians who profited under the colonial system gave their full cooperation—something the colonialists could not have succeeded without.

The Napoleonic Wars forced colonial policy to adopt an aggressive territorial policy. The seizure of French holdings opened the floodgates for a variety of "reasons" to take, seize or claim other Indian territories to the point where Britain eventually directly administered most of India.

2. What was the result of cross-cultural exchange between Indian and Westerners?
On the British side, a group of scholars known as Orientalists emerged possessing great interest in Indian culture and history. These scholars dedicated themselves to unearthing knowledge regarding ancient Indian languages, cultures, and civilizations. The work of these Western scholars has been credited with rediscovering many archeological sites and bringing again to light the grandeur of India's past. These great discoveries then led Indians themselves to study their own past, stimulating a revival of Indian cultural pride.

On the Indian side, many turned to and adopted British or Western culture in general as India became more Westernized. The middle-class, which based its wealth on new commercial or other economic opportunities provided under the British system, often studied Western classics, learned Latin and English and generally conducted themselves in a very British manner. Many went to school in London or studied in the British educational system. Naturally, these individuals were exposed to the philosophical ideals of equality, freedom, democracy, self-determination, etc.

3. In what way did the Revolt of 1857 mark a turning point in Indian / British relations?
Initially relations between Westerners and Indians had been largely based on mutual cooperation thus both profited from the newly budding trade networks. With time, however, British attitudes adopted a much more paternalistic and racist view of India. Many in England and elsewhere spoke of the need to "civilize" India and raise it to Western standards. Naturally, this view presumed that India was not civilized and not, therefore, as good as England or any other Western nation. As attitudes hardened, tension and misperception between Indians, who resented being considered less than civilized, and British, who now considered Indians as inferior.

The Revolt of 1857 signaled the full transition between a relationship based on cooperation and mutual respect for common goals and one that was hierarchical, judgmental, and presumptuous. Atrocities committed by both sides during the Rebellion insured that a moderate voice could never again characterize the terms in which both sides interacted with the other.

4. How did the British contribute to the rise of modern India?
India as a country did not exist before the British system established itself. Those living in India saw themselves not as Indians but as Bengalis, Deccanis, Kashmiris, etc. Regional loyalties dominated because there existed no national identity large enough to link all peoples living on the Indian subcontinent.

With the arrival of the Westerners, however, India as a nation began to take form. Transportation and communication networks connected the various regions to each other. Modern newspapers gave Indians news of others living in far distant parts of India. The English language became a common medium of communication that all educated Indians could use to interact with each other. British territorial acquisition unified parts of India under one administration. British education gave Indians an understanding of the Western concept of nation, national sovereignty, national self-determination and the rights and privileges afforded a nation. The early work of the Orientalists gave India a heritage which Indian intellectuals used to create a national culture and national identity that transcended the regional differences that had divided Indians in the past. And, the British eventually came to serve as a common scourge which required the cooperation of all Indians to overthrow.

Questions For Class Discussion

1. Do you agree with the author that it was unfortunate that "Rajputs, [and] Marathas—saw each other as rivals and indeed as enemies" rather than uniting to defeat the British? Why?
   Arguments agreeing with the author assume that English domination of India until the mid-twentieth century was worse than domination by one of these regional satraps. They may also point out that had they united, not only would the British have been repelled, but the damage done in conflicts between each other would have been avoided.

   Those who disagree with the author may use the argument that using the hindsight of the British takeover is unfair. The British provided stability and order for eighty years before British arrogance damaged relations with the Indians. In fact, the British have even been credited by some for uniting India to the point that it became a single political unit---or the India as it is known today instead of a series of regional kingdoms.

2. During the 1700's, why might have an Indian of average means or less supported the British instead of the ruling dynasty?
   The British established law and order which offered protection against bandits. British trade also brought more jobs and income for the average Indian. And, in the field of soldiering--an important occupation for Indian men--serving on the side of the British was more secure and profitable than on the other side.

3. During the 1700's, why might Indian merchants or other wealthy Indians have supported the British?
   The British Navy offered better protection from pirates than the Portuguese did. The British also expanded local economies with their purchase of cotton, saltpeter, and indigo. Maintaining law and order also allowed trade to continue thus benefiting merchants, agents, and bankers.

4. Some nationalists have contended that British imperialism in India and elsewhere in Asia followed a conscious policy to capture lands through a "divide and conquer" policy. How valid is this view of history?
   Certainly the British used division to gain allies in their attempts to enforce their rule or place an ally on a regional throne. However, divisions among the peoples of India

had already existed for over a thousand years and were certainly not "created" by the British to weaken India. Also, the spread of British control in India actually occurred in piecemeal fashion; usually via action taken only hesitatingly as volatile situations required it.

5. The Manchu takeover of China can be compared with Britain's entrance into India. How did the two roles resemble each other? In what ways did they differ?
Both the British and Manchus ruled vast numbers of people with very few of their own. Both (in the beginning) at least nominally tolerated if not respected the native traditions. Both took advantage of divisions and conflict among the native peoples in their rise to power. And, both used native people in administrative positions.

6. What led British attitudes to shift "from tolerance to arrogance" regarding their Indian colonies?
Knowledge of European history is needed for this one. In the early 1800s, with the defeat of Napoleon, the British emerged as the most powerful nation in Europe. Throughout the early to mid 1800's, Britain also proved remarkably successful through its agricultural and industrial revolutions, powerful navy, etc. At the same time, the 1859 publication of Darwin's *Origin of Species* and the 1871 *Descent of Man* eventually gave Europeans "scientific proof" (Social Darwinism) that the British were superior. (Just a reminder: Darwin did not put forth Social Darwinism, that idea was championed by Herbert Spencer.) See Chapter 14, "Economics and Empire" for further information. All led the British to assume an air of arrogance and to view other civilizations as inferior to themselves.

7. What are some of the positive contributions of British rule in India? What are some of the negative results? Was British rule good or bad for India?
There are many pros associate with British rule, including the expanded economy, uniform laws and education, the introduction of railroads and the telegraph, to name just a few. On the cons side, most of the money from the expanded economy did not stay in India or was spent on British living in India. After 1857, native Indians were treated with disdain and worse for nearly a century by their rulers.

Multiple Choice Questions

1. Which of the following problems did *not* confront the Mughals at the start of the eighteenth century?
   a. A Sikh rebellion
   b. Maratha attacks
   c. weak British leadership
   d. All of the above

2. The first Westerners to arrive in India were the:
   a. Portuguese.
   b. British.
   c. French.
   d. Dutch.

3. In 1650, the Dutch established a base in Sri Lanka by defeating the:
   a. British.
   b. Spanish.
   c. French.
   d. Portuguese.

4. The English, finally won acceptance in India by defeating the Portuguese in a naval battle in sight of the coast of:
   a. Madras.
   b. Goa.
   c. Surat.
   d. Bombay.

5. English relations with Mughal India began with the embassy of:
   a. Robert Clive.
   b. William Hawkins.
   c. Warren Hastings.
   d. Thomas Roe.

6. The first English base established in India was at:
   a. Goa.
   b. Madras.
   c. Surat.
   d. Karachi.

7. Madras was:
   a. the center of French power in India.
   b. an English trading station in Western India.
   c. England's major base in South India.
   d. the Mughal capital.

8. In 1690 the British established a trading station and town on the Hooghly River in the Bengal region. This base became the town of:
   a. Bombay.
   b. Madras.
   c. Calcutta.
   d. Surat.

9. Which of the following Indian cities was not established by the British?
   a. Calcutta
   b. Madras
   c. Bombay
   d. Delhi

10. In 1717 the East Indian Trading Company was given:
    a. the right to collect taxes.
    b. control of South India.
    c. control of Bengal.
    d. the Portuguese trading post in India.

11. What was *not* a problem facing the British East Indian Trading Company as it fought to establish a base in India?
    a. Dealing with Mughal rulers
    b. Fighting the French
    c. Civil unrest
    d. Hindu opposition

12. The center of French power in India was:
    a. Madras.
    b. Goa.
    c. Surat.
    d. Pondicherry.

13. Robert Clive broke the power of the Bengali state at the battle of:
    a. Plassey.
    b. Pondicherry.
    c. Hyderbad.
    d. Agra.

14. Which of the following was *not* a feature in the life of Robert Clive?
    a. Driving the French from India
    b. Defeating the Bengalis
    c. Returning to India in an attempt to reform Company practices
    d. Retiring and becoming a respected member of Parliament

15. Warren Hastings:
    a. defeated the Marathas.
    b. consolidated British power in India.
    c. deposed the last Mughal ruler of India.
    d. made India into a British colony.

16. Which of the following men did not serve as governor-general in India during the late eighteenth century?
    a. Warren Hastings
    b. Richard Wellesley
    c. William Hawkins
    d. Lord Cornwallis

17. Why were the English able to establish so much control over India in the early nineteenth century?
    a. Internal divisions within the Indian states
    b. English rule was milder than native rule
    c. The British brought order to the lands they governed
    d. All of the above

18. Indian culture was made known to England through:
    a. the work of the Orientalists.
    b. Robert Clive's journals.
    c. *The London Times*.
    d. the writings of Dickens.

19. The Indian reaction to British academic study of India was:
    a. disinterest.
    b. the Hindu Renaissance.
    c. jealous hostility.
    d. concern.

20. What was *not* a result of the Orientalist movement in India?
    a. The Hindu Renaissance
    b. The creation of a literate middle class in India
    c. The discovery of much of India's "forgotten" past
    d. British rejection of Indian culture

21. The colonial capital of British India was:
    a. Delhi.
    b. Bombay.
    c. Calcutta.
    d. Madras.

22. In 1833 Parliament:
    a. took control of India.
    b. abolished the East India Company's monopoly in India.
    c. disbanded the East India Company.
    d. opened India to Christian missionaries.

23. After 1835 Parliament decided to:
    a. openly encourage India's interest in its own culture.
    b. encourage Indian interest in Western learning.
    c. stop educating Indians.
    d. suppress the Hindu Renaissance.

24. Which of the following was *not* an important innovation in Indian society introduced by England?
    a. The railroad
    b. The telegraph
    c. The stock market
    d. The press

CHAPTER 14
The Triumph of Imperialism in Asia

Outline Of Main Ideas
- Imperialism and Western dominance—the perspective of the foreign imperialist nations

A. The New Imperialism:
- political and economic domination by technologically advanced industrial-capitalist nations

   i. Conflicting Interpretations
   - social Darwinism; national ambition and competition

   ii. Economics and Empire
   - economic rivalry and competition between the European powers; the "civilizing mission" of the West; the search for new markets
   - Marxist views of surplus capital; Leninism
   - the popularity of adventure among energetic Europeans

B. Imperialism in Asia and Asian Responses
- colonies versus semi-colonial states; the revival and repackaging (modernizing) of the Asian traditions; Western attraction to and lifestyles in Asia
- the development of industry and the rise of national identity among colonial peoples

C. British Imperial India
- the English East India Co.; the Rebellion; the rather slow response of Indian nationalism; direct British rule

i. Modern Growth
- developing transportation networks; exclusive life of overlords; commerce and agriculture; industry

ii. Colonial System
- British pride; the "civilizing mission" of the Europeans; successes: education, law, civil service
- problems: widespread poverty, rising population; economic stratification, fiscal inadequacy
- Indian cooperation and collaboration; British elitism

iii. New Delhi: Indian Summer of the Raj
- the move of the capital from Calcutta to Delhi (1911); the planning of New Delhi; the symbolic meanings of the new capital

iv. The Rise of Indian Nationalism
- thoughts of independence among educated Indians; the early Indian independence movement leaders; the Invasion of Afghanistan (1878), Lhasa
- problems: poverty, political repression; World War I and its impact on India; the emergence of Gandhi; the Amritsar Massacre; the slow British response to Indian demands

D. Colonial Regimes in Southeast Asia

i. The British in Burma and Malaya
- the British supplant the Dutch; the British-Burmese Wars; British colonialization of Burma
- commercialization; agricultural development; Chinese, Indian and British dominance

ii. French, Dutch and American Colonialism
- the French in Indochina; France's police-state rule of the colony; young Ho Chi Minh
- the Dutch in Indonesia; Holland's search and demands for natural resources drive increasing territorial control; oppressive authoritarian rule over Indonesia
- the Americans in the Philippines; development and exploitation of the colony; U.S. democratic idealism; the U.S. colonial government's neglect of the peasantry; independence

iii. Independent Siam
- Thailand as a buffer between British and French interests; Siam's semicolonial status; agriculture and natural resource exports

iv. Overseas Chinese
- Chinese labor and entrepreneurs; the separate Chinese identity; Chinese welcomed by colonialists but resented by indigenous peoples

E. China Besieged
- the Opium War and the resulting Treaty of Nanking; China and semicolonialism; the Arrow War and the burning of the summer palace

i. Traders and Missionaries
- Christian missionaries in China and "gunboat diplomacy"; the Tientsin Massacre (of Catholics); the Sino-French War

ii. Taiping Rebellion
- the limited influence of foreigners on China as a whole; the rise of Hung Hsiu-ch'uan; the rebel capture of Nanking
- factionalism in the rebel ranks; the tremendous destruction of the Taiping rebellion; other contemporary rebellions

iii. Attempts at Reform
- Russian encroachment into Chinese territory and Chinese victory; the "self-strengthening" movement; Beijing's conservative court and the empress dowager Tzu-Hsi

iv. Treaty Ports and Mission Schools
- the rise of Western-dominated treaty port cities; incipient industrialization; Western arrogance and Chinese nationalism
- missionaries: emphasis on religion verses social change; the Westernization of Chinese students; the spread of Western learning; the treaty ports and their relationship to revolutionaries

v. The Boxer Rebellion
- Chinese peasant attacks on Chinese Christians and missions; the Chinese court's support for Boxers; the multi-national expedition and defeat of the Boxers
- the 1911 Revolution and the collapse of dynastic rule

F. Japan Among the Powers

i. Directed Change
- the Meiji Restoration (1868); "strengthen Japan" via borrowing; widespread Westernization among Japanese

ii. Economy and Government
- the Japanese acceptance of industrialization and Westernization as a means to "rich country strong army"; homogeneity and modernization; Japanese agriculture

iii. Japanese Imperialism
- rise of Japanese prestige and power on the world stage; revocation of the unequal treaties; Japanese colonialism: Korea, Taiwan; the Russo-Japanese War (1904); Japanese interests in Korea and Manchuria
- Western admiration for Japan; World War I; Japan's Twenty-one Demands (1915); rising anti-Japanese sentiment on the world stage; development in Japan's colonies

iv. Ito Hirobumi: Meiji Statesman
- Ito's background and life; Ito's role in Korea and assassination (1909); the demise of a moderate voice in Japanese politics

G. Imperialism and Americans in Asia
- American merchants and shipping in Asia; U.S. commodities of trade; American missionary efforts; the British lead, the Americans follow
- U.S. demands for the "Open door"; the American mission to modernize and "civilize" China; the impact and inspiration of Western ideals
- the U.S. Oriental Exclusion Acts; the Californian anti-Chinese riots; the American philosophical debt to China; Chinese responses to American racism

Essay And Discussion Questions

1. What factors led the Western nations to adopt imperialist foreign policies?

   Europe's fragmented condition in the early modern period, in which the continent was divided into separate and independent nation-states, created a strong sense of competition and rivalry as these nations jockeyed with each other for national prestige, status and power. As some European nations, such as Holland, Portugal and later England, began to acquire territories overseas and profit from those territories, other European nations jumped on the band wagon so as not to be left behind.

   Social Darwinism provided an intellectual or theoretical basis for imperialism. Spencer and Huxley applied Darwin's "survival of the fittest" theories to humanity by equating different races and their socio-cultural systems to species of animals and their level of adaptation. Huxley argued that strong ethnic groups dominate those weaker, or less able to adapt, eventually rendering them extinct unless they changed. Thus, adventure-seeking Europeans pursued conquest to illustrate their fitness.

   Economic rivalry and competition and the lure of profits convinced home governments to support imperialism. As described by Marx, Europeans needed colonies to absorb excess capital and to serve as new markets for European goods produced in great quantities. Missionaries flocked to the colonies for converts and to aid in the "civilization" of "heathen" peoples. And, the constant need to defend what one had already claimed insured that imperialists constantly sought new buffers or trade routes.

2. How did imperialism affect the native cultures of the colonized peoples?

   The native cultures that encountered imperialism generally underwent a process of refinement and definition. Western culture formed a clear boundary that delineated

Europeans from native colonized peoples. Even Westernized Indians, Japanese, Vietnamese, etc. found that no degree of education, money or political power gave them full status as British, American or French citizens; culturally they were always refused full status.

As a result, these same leaders often turned to their own traditional cultures, working with it to create a modern culture that would serve as the national culture of a modern nation. By creating a national culture which all Indians, Japanese, or Vietnamese could relate to, these nationalist leaders sought to unify their respective nations and give the nation a cultural identity that would unite the citizenry.

These newly repackaged cultures had to meet the requirements of "modernity." As a result, the traditional cultures of Asia adapted, rejecting some cultural tendencies (such as *sati*, concubinage, etc.) while adopting others (Western-influenced education, dress, etc.).

3. How did Japan's response to imperialism differ from that of China? From that of India?

For a very long time Ch'ing China sought to resist imperialism first by: 1) limiting Western access to China by restricting Westerners to Canton; 2) then, by strengthening itself by borrowing Western military technology (the self-strengthening movement); 3) then, when that failed, by initiating moderate institutional reform designed to give China the same institutions as the West (100 Days Reform); and finally 4) by attacking and killing foreigners in hopes that China's vast numbers could overwhelm the foreigners in China (the Boxer Uprising).

In each of these four failed plans, China sought to resist Western imperialism in order to protect its traditional Confucian socio-political system. After the disastrous results of the Boxer Uprising, however, most Chinese gave up on the Confucian system as a viable option for the 20th century. By the time of the May Fourth Movement, Chinese stridently began rejecting traditional Chinese culture, hoping instead to deal with imperialism via widespread re-education and Westernization.

In Japan, those willing to fight for the Tokugawa socio-political system were few and far between. The majority of Japanese, including the shogun himself, realized that resisting imperialism in defense of the traditional order was a losing cause. As a result,

Japan's commitment to deep and far reaching socio-political reform and widespread Westernization came very soon after Japan was first opened by Perry.

India presents yet another case. There the traditional order, which never achieved the high level of socio-political unity seen in China or even the cultural homogeneity witnessed in Japan, dissolved shortly after the arrival of the Westerners. Resisting imperialism in defense of a traditional order made no sense since there was no traditional order so to speak of. Rather, India comprised of countless regional orders divided up among princes. The caste system did not extend into the political realm and thus insulated from a change in regime. Indians therefore collaborated with British imperialists until a new order, one with British and Indian elements, arose. Only when Indians saw themselves as disadvantaged in the new order did they begin to resist imperialism that they might take control of the new order into their own hands.

Questions For Class Discussion

1. Why might a member of the British middle class desire a post in India or in another of the Asian colonies?
At home, members of the middle class could not likely advance their economic status and could almost never leave the class status they had at adulthood. Class structure was still rather rigid; (some contend it still is). A person's schooling, accent, and background placed them in a certain class for life. Once in India, however, that same person would be seen as British, the rulers of the country, and that person's class status had little relevance. The opportunities in Asia were many. Even a middle class posting would allow a family money for at least two servants and the chance to live like a "little tin god." Those who were very successful could go back to Britain wealthy and purchase a home fit for the gentry.

2. Compare the administrative policies of French and Dutch colonists to those of the English.
The French and Dutch were much more restrictive. The oppressive police state in Vietnam and the rigid denial of native governmental participation of Indonesia had no equivalents among the British colonies in Asia. The policies of the English have been explained in detail in the previous chapters.

3. Given the time frame, why might Japanese imperialism not only have been expected, but even have been considered appropriate and natural?
   Japan wanted to be considered equal with the Western powers and in their attempts to become so adopted many of the West's institutions and behaviors. These included not only industrialization, education and government, but also the prestige of conquering and maintaining colonies. The "new" countries of Italy and Germany were also looking for their "place in the sun" at this time.

4. Assess American activities in China. How do they compare to those of other Western nations?
   Other than a small contingent of troops in the Philippines (see Chapter 16) that brutally put down an attempted independence movement, American actions in Asia were based mainly on improving trade. Although the U.S. did not engage in much military action compared to Britain and France, it did handle its only colony in similarly brutal fashion. It is true that the U.S. championed the "open door" policy concerning China. However, U.S. leaders were in no position to challenge Britain or a combined European force once the other nations refused China's "territorial integrity."

   The Oriental Exclusion Acts tell a great deal of the feelings most U.S. citizens and officials maintained toward Asians.

Multiple Choice Questions

1. As a result of the "Great Mutiny" the East India Company was dissolved and:
   a. England withdrew from India.
   b. native Indians were put in charge of British interests in India.
   c. India officially joined the British empire.
   d. the English army was sent back to England.

2. In 1877 Queen Victoria:
   a. became Empress of India.
   b. established the Second East India Company.
   c. freed India.
   d. visited India.

3. The opening of the Suez Canal:
   a. increased British influence in India.
   b. freed many Englishmen to leave India.
   c. led to a tremendous surge in English immigration to India.
   d. had little effect on the English in India.

4. Before moving the capital to New Delhi, the three major centers of British power in India were:
   a. Calcutta, Bombay, and Delhi.
   b. Madras, Hyderabad, and Bombay.
   c. Calcutta, Bombay, and Madras.
   d. Surat, Karachi, and Bombay.

5. The Indian Civil Service:
   a. administered much of India.
   b. was hopelessly corrupt and inefficient.
   c. governed English investment in India.
   d. was composed largely of Indians.

6. The Viceroy was the:
   a. chief Indian official in India.
   b. ruler of Bengal.
   c. official English governor of India.
   d. administrator of the Royal Treasury in India.

7. British rule in India was known as the:
   a. Second Empire.
   b. Raj.
   c. Imperial holdings.
   d. Great Experiment.

8. In 1911 the capital of India was moved to:
   a. Madras.
   b. Bombay.
   c. Calcutta.
   d. New Delhi.

9. The leading organization behind the rise of Indian nationalism was the:
   a. Hindu Renaissance.
   b. Muslim League.
   c. Janata Party.
   d. Indian National Congress.

10. During the nineteenth and early twentieth centuries England fought wars of conquest in all of the following states except:
    a. Burma.
    b. Tibet.
    c. Cambodia.
    d. Afghanistan.

11. During WWI Indian troops either fought in or were stationed in all of the following areas except:
    a. Europe.
    b. the Suez Canal.
    c. the Mid-East.
    d. China.

12. The Amritsar Massacre:
    a. enjoyed the approval of the majority of the English public.
    b. was caused by Indian nationalists.
    c. drove a wedge between the Indians and the English.
    d. ended the nationalist movement in India.

13. British rule was established in which of the following two countries in Southeast Asia?
    a. Malaya and Thailand
    b. Burma and Indonesia
    c. Thailand and Cambodia
    d. Burma and Malaya

14. The center of Dutch power in Southeast Asia was:
    a. Malaya.
    b. Indonesia.
    c. Siam.
    d. the Philippines.

15. Which of the following is *not* a state in Indochina?
    a. Cambodia
    b. Burma
    c. Vietnam
    d. Laos
16. The colonial ruler of Indochina was:
    a. England.
    b. Holland.
    c. Germany.
    d. France.

17. The United States acquired the Philippines as the result of:
    a. World War I.
    b. the Open Door Policy.
    c. the Spanish-American War.
    d. a treaty with Japan.

18. The Opium Wars were fought between the Chinese and the:
    a. Japanese.
    b. French.
    c. British.
    d. Russians.

19. The Treaty of Nanking ceded what territory to England?
    a. Macao
    b. Kowloon
    c. Singapore
    d. Hong Kong

20. The Meiji Restoration attempted to:
    a. return Japan to its ancient heritage.
    b. cut off all contacts with the West.
    c. modernize Japan.
    d. end Japanese imperial power.

21. Which was not a major Meiji reform?
    a. Reorganizing the government
    b. Industrializing the economy
    c. Discouraging Japanese travel to the West
    d. Introducing a Western legal system

22. The first Japanese imperialistic conquest was in:
    a. China.
    b. Taiwan.
    c. Siberia.
    d. Korea.

23. Ito Hirobumi was:
    a. a Japanese revolutionary.
    b. the general who defeated Russia in 1905.
    c. the deposed ruler of Korea.
    d. a Meiji statesman.

CHAPTER 15
Subjugation, Nationalism, and Revolution in China and India

Outline Of Main Ideas
- China: indigenous and external factors behind the revolution; revolutionary fits and starts
- India: independence and Gandhi; the search for national consciousness

A. China in Decay
   - the Ch'ing regime ignores the results of the Opium War; foreign impatience and war—increasing foreign control in China; Hong Kong and Kowloon; the dominance of domestic affairs over foreign concerns
   - the limits of foreign influence given China's size; the lure of the Chinese market; limited foreign penetration into China's indigenous markets; the impact of Western ideas; China's slow response

   i. "Self-strengthening" and Restoration
      - Tseng and Li: suppression of the Taipings; foreign relations and court factions; China's "self-strengthening" efforts and the Tung Chih Restoration; conservatism at court; rebellions and fiscal drain; the conservative damper on modernization and development; China's suspicion of foreign educated Chinese; military modernization hampered by Ch'ing corruption and conservatism—defeat by Japan

ii. New Humiliations
   - Kang and Liang: Westernization as the way to national strength; the Hundred Days Reform and Tzu Hsi's coup; the continuation of moderate reforms and xenophobic Boxers; Chinese cultural pride

B. Chaos and Warlordism
 - the 1911 Revolution; Sun Yat-sen's party—the Kuomintang

  i. Sun Yat-sen and Yuan Shih-k'ai
   - Sun's background; early revolutionary activities; the Wu Chang Uprising; Sun's political weakness and lack of vision; the Three Principles of the People
   - Yuan's background; Yuan's betrayal of the Republic; foreign support of Yuan; fragmentation of China and subsequent warlordism; Sun responds by rebuilding the party

  ii. The May Fourth Movement
   - Japan's Twenty-one Demands on China; the Versailles agreements and betrayal of China; Chinese demonstrations and boycotts; intellectual ferment; the rise of Chinese extremist parties

  iii. Prominent Figures in the May Fourth Movement
   - Lu Hsun—critic of traditional society; Hu Shih—liberal advocate of Western democracy; Ch'en Tu-hsiu—Mr. Science and Mr. Democracy, and founder of the Chinese communist party

C. India Under Colonial Rule
 - after 1857: Indian culture left alone; British Indian Army

  i. Economic Change
   - industrialization, commercialization, communication, agriculture: tea industry, and tobacco; the development of ports and railways; booming economic development

  ii. The New Middle Class
 - Westernized Indian entrepreneurs and professionals; India's landowning elite
 - India's untouched masses; the peasants and their relationship to markets: indigo workers

- iii. Mass Welfare
  - peasant prosperity and exploitation; comparisons with China: the cotton industry

- iv. Agriculture and Population
  - extensive irrigation projects; uneven prosperity; inadequate agricultural base vis-à-vis the rising population

- v. Some Comparisons
  - the West and Japan compared to China and India

D. The Beginnings of Indian Nationalism
  - Indian anger at the lack of access to power; Ranade / Gokhale and Indian cultural reform; the rise of cultural nationalism
  - the Indian National Congress (1885); Congress demands and British apathy; the Congress' elite nature
  - Curzon: the division of Bengal; Indian boycotts; the All India Muslim League (1926); the Congress split: radical activists as opposed to liberal reformers
  - Morley: concessions

  - i. World War I
    - India's wartime contributions; Congress and Muslim League cooperation

  - ii. Enter Gandhi
    - Gandhian passive resistance and nonviolent protest; Gandhi the holy man; the development among Indians of a political consciousness

  - iii. Postwar Repression
    - the red scare and the Rowlatt Acts (1919); General Dyer and the Amritsar Massacre

Essay And Discussion Questions

1. What were Ch'ing China's attempts to deal with Western imperialism? How did they fare?

   Ch'ing China had a long tradition of dealing with foreign invaders but most of them came from the northern steppes, not from the southern seas. Western imperialism represented a new and powerful threat with which the Chinese had no experience. After failing to incorporate Western merchants into the traditional tributary system, the Ch'ing court established the Canton system. While these arrangements kept Westerners under Ch'ing control initially, dissatisfied foreign demands for open trade eventually led to war—the Opium War—and the treaty port system in which China lost all control over Western merchants. Under the treaty port system it was the foreigners who had control.

Recognizing their military and political weakness vis-à-vis the Western powers, the Ch'ing Court began searching for a way to reestablish dominion over its own country and restore the glory of the traditional China's Confucian system. The Self-Strengthening Movement sought to empower China by adopting many of the West's inventions, including, naval vessels, arsenals, railways, shipyards, telegraphs, artillery, etc. When put to the test (prematurely some would argue), however, these adaptations proved entirely inadequate despite China's apparent advantage on paper.

The failure of the self-strengthers left a vacuum at court which was soon filled by the Reformers led by K'ang Yu-wei. The Reformers sought to empower China via limited Westernization: the adoption of Western institutions such as education, communications, government systems, etc. By juicing up Confucian society with Western institutions, K'ang hoped to rescue the Ch'ing court and traditional Confucian culture from Western dominance. The Hundred-Days Reforms, however, failed as well by alienating conservatives at the Ch'ing court and failing to provide any solid evidence of change.

The failure of the Reformers left the conservatives in sole control of Ch'ing policy, opening the door for court support for the Boxer Uprising. The Boxers rose initially to challenge the role of Chinese Christians in society. Seizing the opportunity, the court steered the Boxers' anger towards Westerners thereby transforming the uprising into an anti-imperialist crusade to attack and drive foreigners from China. The Boxers' eventual failure, however, meant the death for the traditional system since it confirmed the superior firepower of the West and the desperate inability of the Ch'ing court to effectively manage the problem.

2. The 1911 Revolution has often been compared to the May Fourth Movement. How did both represent major turning points in Chinese history?

The 1911 Revolution marks not just the end of the Ch'ing Dynasty but of all dynasties. The dynastic (or imperial or Confucian) socio-political system did not survive the 1911 Revolution, and as a result, the order that had defined China for over two thousand years finally ceased to exist. The emperor, his bureaucracy, the Confucian gentry, the county magistrates, etc. were no longer employed.

Between 1911 and 1919 when the May Fourth Movement officially began, China failed to establish a new order to replace the old Ch'ing order. Warlords and imperialists dominated the socio-political landscape as China descended into chaos. The May Fourth Movement, however, marks the beginnings of nation-wide nationalistic movements in China. For the first time, Chinese from all over China began to march together protesting the way the imperialist nations treated China. At the same time, intellectuals called for a new national culture to replace the Confucian culture. The Movement also marks the beginning point of the two political parties (the Nationalist Party (Kuomintang or KMT) and the Chinese Communist Party (CCP) that would eventually establish a new socio-political order in China.

3. In what ways did India as a whole "prosper" under the British colonial system?
The British provided Indians with a refuge from the chaos and disunion that had swallowed up most of India after the collapse of the Mughal regime. Many Indians preferred British rule because its safety against marauders, its predictable and reasonable legal system, and its mercantile focus helped many of them establish a decent living. Some even became quite wealthy and rose to form a new middle class.

The British also helped unify India to the point that it eventually came to be viewed and self-defined as a single political entity rather than as a series of princely states or regions. The telegraph and mail systems, railways and shipping networks, the media, the English language itself, and the British administration all served to create and unify a country called "India." With time, Indians themselves began to overlook regional identities and consider themselves "Indians."

Under colonial rule India also began a period of rapid and extensive economic development. India's rather impressive level of industrialization and commercialization all got their beginnings under heavy British influence, as did the spread of agricultural development and irrigation, the construction of ports, railways, and roads, and extensive economic prosperity.

4. In what ways did India as a whole "suffer" under the British colonial system?
Despite India's thriving economic development and prosperity, the benefits of this development did not filter out evenly over the whole of society. The vast majority of India's population—the rural farmers—saw little of these changes, despite extensive agricultural development. Many farmers, particularly those engaged in cash crop production for factories, found themselves at the mercy of the market and were devastated when market shifts dropped prices. Others found themselves unable to compete with factories or agricultural enterprises.

India's rising middle class, meanwhile, found itself empowered economically, but completely disenfranchised in the political arena. No level of education, wealth or Westernization could erase the fact that as Indians, they had very few opportunities for advancement in the colonial administration or in politics in general.

British arrogance and disregard for the Indian subjects also came to be a bitter pill for the Indians to swallow. The Amritsar Massacre and other conflicts typify British strong-arm tactics and general unwillingness to negotiate with much empathy.

Questions For Class Discussion

1. Which groups were most impacted by the May Fourth Movement?
While the movement was widespread, it was generally limited to urban settings. Movement leaders tended to be intellectuals writing to other intellectuals or urban groups (such as labor, shop owners, etc.) Rural constituencies were largely neglected for they were not seen are potentially "politically minded."

2. What did Ch'en Tu-hsiu hope to accomplish by issuing his "Call to Youth?"
According to Ch'en, China's traditions and culture prevented it from keeping up with the West. The time had come to throw off the shackles of the past and build a new China. Thus he appealed to the youth who had not been fully tainted with traditional culture.

3. How would Ch'en's "Call" be received by the youth today in this country?
This could lead to lively debate about generational differences. If this question is asked in a college class setting, a generational split--as well as a political one--between -the students may emerge. At the high school level, the teacher will probably have to

play the role of the "old generation" or invite a more experienced colleague to play the part. (Be sure to select one with a good sense of humor.)

4. Compare/contrast the economic changes of India to those of China in the second half of the 1800's.
Both countries experienced change although economic change in India was deeper, more varied, and longer lasting. Changes included the rise of the railroad, telegraph, and steamship industries. Agriculturally the cultivation of tea and tobacco along with an increase in cotton and jute dramatically expanded the economy in India. The same expansion was not seen in China. The reasons for this are that the British controlled one half of India, had hegemony over the other half and used their "influence" to instill these changes whether the Indians wanted them or not. The Chinese government, on the other hand, was at least nominally in control of over 90% of China, and tended to resist change. Change did occur in China, just not to the extent experienced by India, also due to the fact that China already possessed a highly commercialized economy before the arrival of the West. Thus it had less room and need for expansion.

5. Compare China's early reformers to those of India.
Reformers in both countries congregated in cultural centers. They were generally intellectuals who did little to reach the mass peasant population. Neither group called for a violent overthrow or revolution; rather, they wished to work within the system and to continue to absorb Western ideals.

6. As a reformer how was Gandhi different from the other reformers of his day?
Gandhi, though an intellectual (he was trained in London as a lawyer) did more than talk or write about the need to work with and understand the peasantry. He dressed as a holy man and more importantly backed up this dress with the actions of a holy man. This and his use of traditional symbols and values gained the respect and following of huge numbers of the peasant class.

Multiple Choice Questions

1. In 1860, in retaliation for Chinese refusal to honor the terms of the treaties of Nanking and Tientsin, the British and French:
   a. burned the Summer Palace.
   b. took Hong Kong.
   c. burned Canton.
   d. killed the Emperor.

2. The Taiping Revolt was put down by:
   a. Tzu Hsi.
   b. Prince Kung.
   c. Tseng Kuo-fan and Li Hung-chang.
   d. Tso Tsung-t'ang and Tzu Hsi.

3. In 1894 China was defeated and forced to sign the Treaty of Shiminoseki by:
   a. Japan.
   b. England.
   c. Russia.
   d. Germany.

4. As the result of the Russo-Japanese War of 1905, Japan took over Russia's interest in:
   a. Korea.
   b. Manchuria.
   c. the treaty ports.
   d. Siberia.

5. During the late 1890s the impetus behind the modernization movement in China was:
   a. Kuang-hsü.
   b. K'ang Yu-wei.
   c. Tzu Hsi.
   d. Pu Yi.

6. One impediment to reform in China was:
   a. the military.
   b. Prince Kung.
   c. Tzu Hsi.
   d. Pu Yi.

7. In 1911 the Ch'ing dynasty fell and was replaced by a government led by:
   a. Mao Tse-tung.
   b. Sun Yat-sen.
   c. Harry Soong.
   d. Liang Ch'i-ch'ao.

8. Sun Yat-sen spent much of his life in the West, living for a time in all of the following places except:
   a. Russia.
   b. England.
   c. Hong Kong.
   d. Hawaii.

9. The May 4th Movement had strong support among China's:
   a. military.
   b. peasants.
   c. intellectuals.
   d. warlords.

10. The two major political parties to emerge after the May 4th Movement were the:
    a. Radicals and the Communist Party.
    b. Kuomintang and the May 4th Movement.
    c. Liberation Party and the Kuomintang.
    d. Kuomintang and the Communist Party.

11. The most prominent of all the modern Chinese writers was:
    a. Ts'ai Yuan-p'ei.
    b. Lu Hsun.
    c. Sun Yat-sen.
    d. Ch'en Tu-hsiu.

12. The Indian middle class was largely concentrated in:
    a. Bengal.
    b. the port cities.
    c. Delhi.
    d. South India.

13. The general Indian attitude toward modernization was:
    a. resistance.
    b. suspicion.
    c. acceptance.
    d. indifference.

14. Under British rule peasant life:
    a. probably improved.
    b. probably got worse.
    c. remained unchanged.
    d. was totally disrupted.

15. Under the British, massive irrigation projects were begun in:
    a. Bengal.
    b. Assam.
    c. Punjab.
    d. Orissa.

16. Nationalism first appeared among the Indian:
    a. aristocracy.
    b. Westernized middle class.
    c. military.
    d. peasantry.

17. One reason for the rise of Indian nationalism was:
    a. England's exploitation of India's natural resources.
    b. Indian frustration at being denied participation in the colonial government.
    c. the cruel harshness of British rule.
    d. England's attempt to impose Christianity on India.

18. Under Gandhi the Congress Party:
    a. became aggressively militant.
    b. developed a following among the peasantry.
    c. expelled the Communists.
    d. became an exclusively Hindu movement.

19. Which of the following men was not associated with the Congress Party?
    a. Gandhi
    b. Nehru
    c. Mohammed Ali Jinnah
    d. Ram Mohum Roy

CHAPTER 16
The Struggle for Asia, 1920–1945

Outline Of Main Ideas

A. Colonialism in Southeast Asia
- the slow expansion of colonialism in Southeast Asia; the slow growth of nationalism; widespread collaboration; the Thai exception

  i. The Plantation System
  - industrialization's demands for plantation products; the plantation itself; rubber, sugar, rice

  ii. The Rise of Southeast Asian Nationalism
  - Spanish and American influence in the Philippines; the rise of cultural identities; the rise of elite nationalist parties; prewar nationalists: Ho Chih-Minh, the lustrado, Sukarno, Burmese nationalists, Thai nationalists

B. India Moves Towards Independence
- Gandhi and his program

  i. Gandhi and Mass Action
  - Gandhi's background; Indian strikes and British repression (the Amritsar Massacre, 1919); Indian noncooperation and nonviolent protest; the boycott of British goods; broad-based Indian nationalist movements

ii. Hindus and Muslims: Protest and Elections
   - the Hindu-Muslim split; Jinnah; the effects of the world depression in India; the salt protest; violent demonstrations; elections; World War II; Churchill's fight against independence; Congress leaders jailed by the British; the rise of Jinnah

iii. Retrospect
   - the slow British response to Indian demands for independence; the British legacy in India

C. China in the 1920s and 1930s
- China divided by warlords and regionalism; devastating natural and manmade disasters; development in Manchuria; industry in China as a whole

   i. Marxism and Soviet Help
      - the May Fourth Movement and Marxism; the (First) United Front: the Chinese Communist Party and the Nationalist (Kuomintang) Party; the role of Comintern in Chinese politics; the Northern Expedition; Chiang Kai-shek; Chinese nationalism and violence

   ii. The Nanking Decade
      - the Nationalist's anti-communist extermination campaigns; the communists escape on the Long March; the Tsunyi Conference and Mao's leadership; Yenan
      - Chinese national development under the Nationalist Party; Soong family connections to the Party; taxes and corruption; Nationalist fascism; neglect of the rural areas; the Japanese invasion

   iii. Shanghai: The Model Treaty Port
      - the bastion of dissent; China's cultural center and political center of ferment; the largest port and commercial center; China's largest industrial center
      - the Western presence and dominance of Shanghai; "in China but not of it"; Shanghai's role in stimulating anti-foreign sentiment and resentment

D. Japan from 1920 to 1941
   - World War I and the profits gained from it; free expression and the rise of militarism; internationalism and the Siberian expedition

- universal male suffrage (1925); the Peace Preservation Law (1925); the Taisho Democracy

    i. Growing Influence of the Military
- the rising power of the Japanese military; the Great World Depression and its affect on Japan; the Japanese admiration for fascism; Japanese Manchurian interests and Manchukuo
- the military domination of Japan's civilian government; the persecution of "leftism"; the anti-Comintern Pact; Japanese as opposed to European -fascism; the Diet

    ii. Japan on the Eve of World War II
- Hitler's nonaggression pact with the Soviets; the Tripartite Pact; the U.S. embargo; Pearl Harbor; Japan's search for resources in Southeast Asia; realism verses self-confidence among Japanese leaders

E. The War in China
- the conflict between China and Japan over Manchuria

    i. The Failure of the United Front and the Fall of Nanking
- the kidnapping of Chiang and the (Second) United Front; the Marco Polo Bridge Incident (1937); Chinese resistance to Japanese aggression; the rape of Nanking

    ii. Mao's Guerrilla Strategy
- Chungking and the Nationalist Party; the Chinese communists and guerrilla strategy; popular support for Mao's guerrillas; moderate communist reforms; Mao's anti-Japanese activities; the Maoist ideal of "art serving politics"; Maoism; northern verses southern Chinese resistance; Japanese atrocities in China

    iii. Chungking: Beleaguered Wartime Capital
- Chungking's natural defenses; the transport of factories and libraries to Chungking; corruption, isolation, inflation, demoralization, thought control and paranoia

F. Japan in the Pacific and Southeast Asia
- Pearl Harbor and the U.S. entry into the war; early Japanese victories and atrocities; the Japanese sense of superiority and racism; the significantly high level of Japanese technology
- the U.S. internment camps for Japanese-Americans; Japan's Greater East Asian Co-Prosperity Sphere
- the Battle of Midway; U.S. island hopping and fierce Japanese resistance

G. Burma and India
- the seesaw fight for Burma; jungle warfare; the British defense of India; Subhas Chandra
- Japanese vulnerability; Hiroshima and Nagasaki; Russia's entry into the anti-Japanese war; the Japanese surrender

Essay And Discussion Questions

1. What made nationalism in Thailand different from that in most other Southeast Asian countries?
   A few unique advantages led to the rather early advent of nationalism in Thailand. A long and glorious heritage insured that most of the country spoke Thai and subscribed to the dominant Thai culture, thus making Thailand quite homogenous compared to some of its neighbors such as Laos which contained a vast spectrum of tribal and linguistic distinctions. As a result, the Thais maintained a strong national identity, both of their country as Thailand, and of themselves as Thai people.

   Geopolitically, Thailand also sat at the border between the British and French spheres of influence thus allowing Thailand to remain neutral as a buffer zone between the two. Very capable Thai monarchs insured that neither European power gained any advantage in his country while he initiated modernizing reforms. Thus, the Thais were able to strengthen their own identity and political order while striving to preserve it from the eroding influence of imperialism.

2. How did World War II affect Asia's nationalistic movements?
   At the start of World War II in Asia, the imperial army of Japan invaded several Asian countries and then overthrew their colonial regimes. Although the Japanese did not replace these colonialist powers with independent, indigenous governments or even

regimes that were less oppressive, having the colonial governments gone for just a few years gave local nationalists a glimpse of what the future might hold.

The war in Europe also affected the status quo by allowing nationalists to exact promises out their former colonial masters in repayment for contributions to the war effort. In some areas, such as India, colonial rule did not leave but became harsher under martial law, thus giving nationalists greater cause for resistance after the war. Also, nationalist groups that had long been banned and suppressed by the colonial regimes flourished under Japanese rule. The Japanese had spread themselves too thin and could not subdue nationalist activities to the extent that the colonialist police could. Thus, by the end of the war, many of these groups had not only organized themselves, increased their numbers and galvanized popular support, they had also mastered guerrilla tactics and formulated a socio-political program for change.

World War II also had the effect of weakening some contenders while strengthening others, thus tipping the balances against the status quo before the war. France, Holland and Britain in the post-war period faced the awesome task of reconstructing their own countries and thus, despite early efforts to reestablish colonial control over their colonies, did not possess the strength to reassert themselves. In China, the Nationalist government emerged from the war years a tattered shadow of its former self, while its communist rivals had never been so strong.

3. Why did Japan's Greater East Asian Co-Prosperity Sphere fail to catch on and ignite the interest of other anti-imperialist nationalists? Why did the nationalists fight on the side of their colonial masters?

Not all Asian nationalists fought on the side of the Allies. Most did, however, despite the logic of Japan's proposed program for Asia. Japan defended its invasion of East and Southeast Asia by claiming that the West had dominated Asia long enough and that it was time Asians stood up, ousted imperialism, and regained control of Asia. Japan promised that by providing technological, industrial, and organizational skills to other Asian nations in return for natural resources, Asia would become a powerful economic block able to compete with Europe on equal footing.

In reality, however, Japanese treatment of the native peoples they conquered showed equal or higher levels of cultural arrogance vis-à-vis that displayed by the colonial powers. Failing to recognize the significance of local nationalism, Japanese imperial troops sought to suppress rather than coopt it. Any resistance against Japan met with brutal force meant to intimidate, but which only infuriated local peoples all the more.

Also, although Japan promised technology and industrial support, her energies were too consumed by the war effort to allow her to carry through with the goods. As a result, natural resources flowed to Japan with little in return—once again alienating the local populations.

4. How did Maoist strategy serve the communist rise to power?
After successfully leading the communists through the Long March to Yenan, Mao initiated a plan by which he hoped to make the communists national contenders for political power. From their remote base in Yenan, the communists orchestrated anti-Japanese raids via organized and trained guerrilla fighters. With the Nationalist government passively seated in the mountains of Sichuan, patriotic Chinese interested in actively resisting Japanese aggression had to link up with the communists.

Mao also conducted moderate social reforms, asking landlords to reduce rents, for example, in order to allow peasants more time to fight the Japanese. Rural medical treatment, education, and literacy programs all served to corroborate Mao's commitment to the peasantry. The Red Army, comprised of peasants recruited full time, treated other peasants with respect and kindness, even paying for food acquired from them. As a result, popular support swelled among the peasantry.

Driving this organizational frenzy was a small army of communist cadre who had been thoroughly and meticulously trained for the task. Moving from place to place and creating communist cell organizations in the villages, these cadre eventually succeeded in bringing nearly 100 million under communist organization. Maoist thought glued it all together by providing a vision for a new, stronger China and a reformed countryside where all had a decent standard of living. Maoism also, however, required total and impassioned commitment to the political and ideological dictates of the Party.

Questions For Class Discussion

1. What changes did the plantation system bring to Southeast Asia? Consider developments involving: demographics, the peasantry, economics, traditional lifestyles, and the environment.

Demographics. An influx of foreign labor from India and Ceylon to areas on the western coast and Chinese labor to the eastern side (Indonesia, Philippines, and to a lesser extent Vietnam) raised population densities in these areas. Most were brought in by western companies or came on their own in search of economic opportunity.

Economics. The economy of the Southeast Asian states expanded and the production of crops increased. However, trade—-the basis of the economy—-did not change.

Peasants. The peasants received little from the expanded economy as most profits went to Westerners or a few indigenous businessmen. Even the great demand for rice, a crop not dependent on imported labor or part of the plantation system did little to help the majority of peasants. Though peasants were vital to the expansion of rice growth they did not have the capital required for seed, and equipment. Thus most became tenants (the lucky ones) or laborers (the majority). An important aspect of the expanded economy is that it did provide jobs.

Traditional lifestyles. This differed greatly from country to country. The Philippines witnessed the most dramatic change due to the length of time Spanish involvement and to the Social Darwinist beliefs of the Americans. Indonesia and Malay experienced little change having been left alone to their own traditional culture. Most natives were not worried about being overwhelmed by the Western powers but by other Asian powers, particularly China and India, whose influences had been fairly strong for a millennium and who, with the new influx of laborers and merchants (the rice export trade was run mainly by Chinese) were most likely to implement changes.

Environment. This has only become a concern recently. The export trade in hardwoods and the use of chemical fertilizers have had major effects on the environment.

(This question could be used by placing students in groups and giving them choices as to which sections they prefer to answer. A trip to the library would be helpful.)

2. How can we account for the relatively late start (1920's-30's) of nationalist movements in most of Southeast Asia?
   The most obvious reason lies with the fact that "colonialism came late to most of Southeast Asia" as the author points out in the beginning of Chapter 16. When this factor is combined with the assertion that "Western colonialism unified areas in much

of Southeast Asia that had never been unified before, politically or socially" it is easy to see that there was no major impetus for nationalism until the 1930's. Other reasons are similar to those seen in India and China. The Western power(s) did not threaten traditional culture. Many people admired what the West offered (militarily and industrially mainly) and the expanded economies brought by the West meant jobs and a middle class which in return supported the West.

3. What events made the 1920's a fertile period for Chinese revolutionary groups such as the Kuomintang and the Chinese Communist Party?
The May 4th Movement and Social Darwinism generated a nation-wide concern among educated Chinese for China's future. At the same time, warlordism threatened the integrity and survival of the country. Civil wars and natural disasters made worse by the neglect of the infrastructure generated energies that nationalists were able to harness and mold into these two parties—both of which promised to usher in a new era of peace, prosperity and stability.

4. How is it that both democracy and militarism could expand in Japan from 1889 until the early 1930's?
Many Japanese officials believed that following the Western pattern of colonialism was the only way to be considered equal by the West. The influence of the new and powerful Prussia/Germany also made an impression on a Japan looking for a Western model. And, of course the much admired work of Benito Mussolini in Italy was very influential in Japan as it was in much of the world. While this transpired, the West itself engaged in the heavy promotion of democracy for Japan and for itself. England, for example, in step-by-step process gave all men the right to vote through the late 1800's and early 1900's culminating in universal male suffrage and suffrage for women over 30 in 1918.

5. Was the war between Japan and the United States inevitable?
It certainly would have been very difficult to work out a diplomatic solution. Feeling cornered by the U.S.'s embargo, Japan figured the only way to get out from under the thumb of Western domination was to assert their own colonial system: The Greater East Asian Co-Prosperity Sphere. The Japanese did not trust the West because of the way they had been treated in previous dealings with the West (i.e. the Treaty of Portsmouth, the Twenty-One Demands and the refusal to include a clause against racism in the League of Nations covenant). U.S. demands that Japan completely withdraw from China before the embargo be lifted were even acknowledged by U.S.

officials as unacceptable to the Japanese. Japan had invested too much in China for any Japanese leader to simply give it up. Nevertheless, one could argue that nothing is inevitable.

Multiple Choice Questions

1. The first Southeast Asian country to be colonized by a Western power was:
   a. Vietnam.
   b. Burma.
   c. the Philippines.
   d. Siam.

2. Which Southeast Asian country escaped Western colonization?
   a. Indonesia
   b. Cambodia
   c. Laos
   d. Thailand

3. The chief source of colonial income in Southeast Asia was:
   a. the area's mines.
   b. the plantation system.
   c. trade with the cities.
   d. taxes.

4. The Philippines were first colonized by the:
   a. Spanish.
   b. Dutch.
   c. French.
   d. Germans.

5. Emilio Aquinaldo was the:
   a. last Spanish governor of the Philippines.
   b. Spaniard who conquered the Philippines.
   c. leader of the Philippines independence movement.
   d. first democratically elected ruler of the Philippines.

6. Gandhi opposed British rule with:
   a. terrorism.
   b. political action in England.
   c. non-violent action.
   d. legal test in the courts.

7. One of the many symbols for Gandhi's independence movement was the:
   a. cobra.
   b. bow.
   c. begging bowl.
   d. spinning wheel.

8. In the 1940's a major opponent to Indian independence was:
   a. Lord Mountbatten.
   b. Winston Churchill.
   c. Parliament.
   d. George VI.

9. The Soviet advisor to the Communist Chinese and the Kuomintang was:
   a. Beria.
   b. Borodin.
   c. Molatov.
   d. Andropov.

10. Which of the following became the KMT's helmsman after Sun Yat-Sen:
    a. Mao Tse-tung.
    b. Lu Hsun.
    c. Pu Yi.
    d. Chiang Kai-shek.

11. In 1927 Chiang Kai-shek turned his soldiers against:
    a. the Japanese.
    b. his former communist allies.
    c. the population of Shanghai.
    d. the Westerners living in the treaty ports.

12. At the 1922 Washington Naval Conference Japan agreed to:
    a. withdraw from Korea.
    b. help pay for WWI.
    c. limit its presence in Manchuria.
    d. limit its navy.

13. The 1889 Japanese Constitution was modeled on that of:
    a. the United States.
    b. Prussia.
    c. France.
    d. England.

14. In 1940 Japan signed an alliance with:
    a. Russia.
    b. England and the United States.
    c. Germany and Italy.
    d. China.

15. Prior to WWII the United States:
    a. was a Japanese ally.
    b. supplied vital war materials to Japan.
    c. had broken relations with Japan.
    d. had major investments in Japanese oil.

16. Mao based his power upon support of China's:
    a. intellectuals.
    b. cities.
    c. peasants.
    d. military.

17. For most of WWII the Kuomintang government was:
    a. besieged in Chungking.
    b. used to fight a guerrilla war against Japan.
    c. very effective.
    d. battling the local warlords.

18. The turning point of the war in the Western Pacific came in 1942 with the battle of:
    a. Midway.
    b. Guadalcanal.
    c. the Coral Sea.
    d. Wake Island.

CHAPTER 17
Revival and Revolution in Japan and China

Outline Of Main Ideas

A. The Revival of Japan
- extensive destruction as a result of the war; the peaceful transfer of power to the U.S.

   i. Occupation and Americanization
   - the popularity of the U.S. among Japanese; U.S. anti-fascist and anti-militarist reforms; U.S. efforts at decentralization and land reform; the pro-democracy reforms: a new constitution, the emperor, the armed forces
   - the Cold War and U.S. policy changes; the U.S.-Japan Security Treaty

   ii. Economic and Social Development
   - Japan's rapid economic growth; the quality and quantity of products
   - successes: democracy, education, social harmony and equity, the avoidance of heavy military spending
   - problems: "high pressure" society; population density; *eta* and Korean minorities; Japan's hierarchical society and the role of women

   iii. Japan's International Role
   - Japan's international political reluctance and self consciousness; its future potential; stringent pollution controls; population controls; urbanization; the distinctive Japanese culture

iv. Tokyo and the Modern World
- the world's largest city; the Imperial Palace; Tokyo's blend of modernity and tradition

v. Japan's Relations with its Former Enemies
- Russia and the Kurile Islands; the U.S. and issues over nuclear testing; the U.S.' "reverse course"; Japan's entrance into the United Nations (1956); popular Japanese resistance to U.S. political pressure; the textbook controversies; Westernization and Japanese identity

B. China in Revolution

i. Communist Strength and Kuomintang Weakness
- the Japanese occupation of China; the decline of the Nationalist government and the rise of the Chinese communists; the Maoist peasant revolution; civil war; the founding of the People's Republic of China (PRC); Mao's "mass line"

ii. Reconstruction and Politicization
- Taiwan; PRC land reform; PRC control over outlying regions; the period of "A Hundred Flowers Bloom"; the communist use of political campaigns

iii. The Great Leap Forward
- the communes; the Great Leap Forward; the Great Leap's failure and massive starvation; the rise of moderate rule in China

iv. The Sino-Soviet Split
- Moscow's dissatisfaction with Mao; the withdrawal of Soviet support; Russian-Chinese border clashes; issues of disagreement and points of contention; U.S.-China détente

v. The Cultural Revolution
- Mao's objectives for the revolution and political comeback; "enemies" identified and attacked; "better red than expert"; education and "reeducation"; the "sent down youth" ordered to the countryside; the emergence of Red Guards; widespread violence; military intervention; attacks on high officials; the anti-urban bias of the revolution; social controls; rural industrialization; egalitarianism; Mao and traditional Chinese culture

  vi. Chiang Ch'ing and the Gang Of Four
- traditional Chinese views about women in politics; Chiang Ch'ing's background; Chiang Ch'ing in the Cultural Revolution

  vii. China After Mao
- the fall of Chiang Ch'ing; the slow reversal of isolation; the rise of Teng Hsiao-p'ing (Deng Xiaoping); the responsibility system and free market; China's economic development; socialism verses capitalism; Mao's mistakes; the decline of ideological commitment in China

  viii. Achievements and the Future
- successes: agriculture, nuclear energy, health care, population control, economic gains, literacy, rising living standard
- problems: pollution, economic disparity
- modernization programs; liberalization of women

  ix. Renewed Demands for Liberalization
- the pro-democracy movement (1989); the Peking Massacre; Tibet and Mongolia; religion and religious freedom in China
- the future: Teng's demise; unemployment; corruption; high but uneven growth rates

C. Taiwan
- the aborigines and the "Taiwanese"; Japanese control of Taiwan; Taiwan as a refuge for the defeated Nationalist government; Nationalist repression of native Taiwanese
- Taiwan's economic growth; political liberalization; issues concerning the reunification of China and Taiwan

D. Hong Kong
- Hong Kong the British colony; the flood of refugees entering Hong Kong; trade and finance; Hong Kong's economic growth; Hong Kong's return to Chinese sovereignty; Hong Kong and the PRC

Essay And Discussion Questions

1. What did the U.S. occupation of Japan aim to accomplish and how did it proceed to do so?
   The occupation had two primary objectives immediately after the war: to weaken socio-political institutions or entities that contributed to Japanese militarism, and to strengthen socio-political institutions or entities that strengthened democracy. By way of accomplishing the first task, occupation authorities broke up the *zaibatsu*, purged leaders and managers too closely associated with Japanese fascism, dismantled the military machine, tried Japanese war criminals, and so forth.

   To support democracy, SCAP released Japan's political prisoners, decentralized the central government giving more power to local administrations, initiated land reform, revitalized the electoral and party systems, promulgated a new constitution, constructed a new educational system, etc.

   With the beginning of the Cold War, these U.S. objectives blurred somewhat as the SCAP attempted to curb left-wing activism. Many of the leaders and managers initially purged for their links to fascism were recalled and given positions of leadership once again. Freedom of the press, which had been granted as a means of supporting democratic ideals, came under strict censorship. And, among other things, the freedom of political parties was curtailed-.

2. How has Confucianism served modern Japan? How has it created problems for modern Japanese?
   Traditional Confucian ideals continue to play an important role in Japanese society and contribute to the overall success of the nation. The Confucian concern for education insures that the Japanese not only claim the world's highest literacy rate, but also place the most emphasis on it. Japanese students devote most of their waking hours to school and study but stand to reap tremendous rewards if they excel.

   Confucian group responsibility and identity foster one of the world's lowest crime rates. Criminal behavior places great shame on one's family thus serving to dissuade illegal activity. The Confucian emphasis on social harmony functions in a similar way to maintain order in society from the level of the family on up. Everyone in Japan fits into a hierarchy that possesses some leverage over him or her and uses it to prevent discord and conflict which might result in a loss of face.

On the other hand, these same social hierarchies tend to place individuals under tremendous social pressure. Individuality and personal freedom are little appreciated and draw to oneself unwanted attention. Japan's hierarchical nature, while insuring that conflict does not erupt does little to resolve the problems causing friction in the first place. Women and the young have little recourse against social pressures exerted by those at the top of the hierarchies. The *eta*, Japan's lowest class faces racist policies and attitudes in virtually every sphere of life due to this hierarchical nature of Japanese society.

3. What were the results of the Cultural Revolution?

Mao ostensibly launched the Cultural Revolution to save the revolution from bureaucratization, corruption and capitalism which had crept into China after the failed Great Leap Forward. It also promised to usher Mao back into the political mainstream by circumventing his political opposition with an appeal directly to the people. Maoist China had long been one of the world's most politicized nations. Political campaigns insured that all kept abreast of the political winds from the capital, kept up on their study of Marxist, Leninist, and Maoist Thought, and kept themselves pure from anything that might taint their political dossiers.

The Cultural Revolution, however, unleashed social tensions that even Mao did not foresee and virtually destroyed the country. Egalitarianism and political correctness were pushed to extremes as Red Guard factions fought pitched battles with one another in effort to prove their "redness." High officials, parents, teachers and anyone with "authority," tainted with "Western decadence" or defiled by "feudal" culture, were denounced, beaten, jailed or killed outright. Most of China's official systems collapsed: including education, transportation and communications.

By the time Mao finally died and the Cultural Revolution officially ended, the Chinese people were exhausted and disillusioned with politics. The military had been called in to suppress the Red Guards, who were then sent to live in the countryside to get them out of the way. Naturally, many felt betrayed by the Party and enthusiasm for the communist revolution turned into concern for one's own personal livelihood. Most urban Chinese had been affected and the country required a great deal of healing. Politically, the communist party no longer had the luxury or prestige to call for national sacrifice as had consistently occurred under Mao. Nor did political campaigns, propaganda, and social control have the same effect. Most Chinese had had enough.

4. What distinguishes the Deng Era from the Mao Era?
   Under Mao, politics and ideology drove most other concerns. Mao's vision and leadership had propelled the Chinese communists from the verge of extinction to national power, convincing him that China's fate depended on him alone. As a result, Mao thought big. To Mao, the revolution that brought the communists to power did not just represent a means to an end, but the secret to continued success. The revolutionary experience empowered and strengthened Chinese while rooting out "feudal" or backward elements of society that obstructed China's march into a bright future. Mao thus initiated political campaigns which required that "good" people struggle against "bad" ones. He also restructured the class system placing "good" classes at the top, which included first and foremost the poor peasants, and the "bad" classes at the bottom, i.e., the landlords. The Great Leap Forward intended to accelerate China's development past that of the U.S. and England. Later, the Cultural Revolution focused on restoring the ideological and political purity characterizing the Party in its earlier days.

   By the time of Deng, Chinese people had become disinterested in politics or ideology. Deng, himself a foreign-trained economist, emphasized economic development as opposed to political or ideological purity. To Deng, ideology meant little when compared to the bottom line. As a result, Deng's regime has concentrated on bringing about the Four Modernizations, on providing market features and incentives to stimulate productivity, on closing down inefficient state enterprises and turning them over to private hands, and so forth. None of this would have been tolerated by Mao, but then again, nor would Mao's dogmatic tactics have been endured by Deng had he the power to determine otherwise.

Questions For Class Discussion

1. The Cold War is over. Should the United States close its military bases in Japan? What arguments can be made for or against such a measure? (Think of the possible ramifications in Japan, and greater Asia.)
   Most Japanese still support maintaining American troops in Japan. If the troops were sent home the Japanese would be required to build up their self-defense force. That action might not break the law set forth in Article 9 but it would certainly bend it. Many Japanese still do not trust the military and wonder how much "build-up" would satisfy it. This problem also concerns many other Asian nations that fully remember the occupation of their lands by the Japanese. Another problem is that the Japanese

government has just offered an official apology (summer 1995) to these nations concerning their actions during World War II. The combination of these two problems worry many Asians; they would much rather have the Americans stationed there. Also, a Japanese military buildup would also give an excuse to many other Asian nations to expand their own militaries, which would most likely lead to even more political tensions which tend to strain over militarization issues.

(Another interesting aspect of the Japanese constitution are Articles 14 and 24 which guarantee women's equality in strong language. They state in part: "the equal rights of husband and wife" and "with regard to choice of spouse, property rights, inheritance, choice of domicile, divorce and other matters pertaining to marriage and the family, laws shall be enacted from the standpoint of individual dignity and the essential equality of the sexes." Even more remarkable is the fact that Article 24 (above) and Article 14 were written by a twenty-two year old woman: Beate Sirota. Sirota was born in Vienna but spent the ages five to fifteen living in Japan before immigrating to the United States. Because of her fluency in Japanese she was given a post in the Occupation.)

2. Ex-Senator Paul Tsongas, an American politician, once stated, "the Cold War is over—Japan won." Assess the validity of this statement.
If the "war" between the United States and the Soviet Union can be defined as a battle between economic systems to see which will emerge most ready to enter the twenty-first century then Senator Tsongas' argument has some validity. Of course the war cannot be reduced to simple economics but it does make for interesting class discussion.

3. Why, despite tremendous economic, industrial, and military advantages, did the Kuomintang fail to maintain control over China?
(Information can also be found in Chapter 16—The Nanking Decade.) Answers to this question are legion. The KMT never truly had control of the country. Warlords, the Communists, Party factions and military cliques, in addition to Japanese militarists, insured that the KMT's first energies were devoted to survival rather than national construction. Also, paranoid of being infiltrated by other groups, the KMT viewed non-KMT organizations with suspicion, thus alienating potentially useful allies and broad segments of the population. Overzealous police, propaganda, and anti-insurgent efforts also alienated social groups. Ineffective policies of tax collection and rural reform turned the peasantry against the Party. Intellectual crackdowns and censorship

did the same to the urban educated classes. Economically, the depression took its toll but the Japanese invasion and its subsequent destruction destroyed what the KMT had built. By the time it emerged from the war the Party was both demoralized and corrupt--incapable of building national unity against the communists who had gained the momentum. Thus, despite the KMT's apparent advantages on paper, it proved unable to maintain control.

(An outstanding firsthand account of village China during World War II is Murphey's *Fifty Years of China to Me—Personal Reflections of 1942-1992* published by the Association for Asian Studies, Inc. Ann Arbor, Michigan.)

4. In what ways was Mao successful? In what ways was he unsuccessful?
Mao was obviously successful as the leader of the Revolution of 1949. His efforts thrust a tiny, malnourished and hunted band of communists into the upper echelons of national power. He also brought peace and stability to China after years of warfare and turmoil. After taking power, however, Mao's vision and foresight failed him as the Great Leap Forward and the Cultural Revolution produced unwanted consequences of monumental proportions.

5. What does the future hold for communism in China? Will China's communist government fall in a violent protest/civil war? Will it experience something like Czechoslovakia's Velvet Revolution? Will China stay its course or revert to a stronger communism? Or, will China become a military dictatorship?
Any educated guess is probably as good as anyone else's. Good answers should reveal knowledge of China's current and recent history. Students may even employ the author's suggestion that China will probably take a wait-and-see approach for the next few years to learn what it can from Hong Kong.

Multiple Choice Questions

1. Supreme Commander Allied Powers (SCAP) was the:
   a. allied occupation government of Japan after WWII.
   b. allied war crimes tribunal held in Japan after WWII.
   c. allied plans for the invasion of Japan.
   d. U.N. force that occupied Japan after WWII.

2. The commander of U.S. forces in Japan after WWII was:
   a. George Marshall.
   b. George Patton.
   c. J.P. Davis.
   d. Douglas MacArthur.

3. The American occupation of Japan after WWII was:
   a. harsh and vindictive.
   b. mild and supportive.
   c. resented by most Japanese.
   d. hindered by Russian interference.

4. The *zaibatsu* were Japanese:
   a. worker associations.
   b. military police.
   c. industrial cartels.
   d. religious orders.

5. Among the reforms introduced by the occupational government of Japan after WWII were:
   a. land reform.
   b. educational reform.
   c. democratic reform.
   d. all of the above.

6. One reason for the rapid Japanese recovery after WWII was:
   a. the wise use of Japan's massive mineral and energy resources.
   b. the heavy use of resources stolen from southeast Asia during the war.
   c. the installation of new machinery and industrial plants.
   d. the reconstruction of Japan's military.

7. After WWII, the Emperor was:
   a. tried as a war criminal.
   b. retained in a ceremonial role.
   c. deposed.
   d. given a more active role in government.

8. Which is *not* one of the achievements of Japan during the years since WWII?
   a. The control of population growth
   b. Increased industrial output
   c. The reconstruction of a blue water navy
   d. Extensive pollution control

9. The most powerful political party in post-war Japan has been the:
   a. Socialist Party.
   b. Liberal Democratic Party.
   c. Nationalist Party.
   d. Republican Party.

10. Which was *not* an advantage enjoyed by the Kuomintang in their struggle with the Communists during the years after WWII?
    a. A large army
    b. Control of China's cities
    c. Support of the United States
    d. Support of China's peasantry

11. With the Communist victory in 1949, Chiang Kai-shek and the Kuomintang government:
    a. fled to the United States.
    b. fled to Taiwan.
    c. were executed by Mao.
    d. went into exile in Japan.

12. The Great Leap Forward was Mao's attempt to:
    a. reorganize China's urban life
    b. rapidly industrialize China
    c. open contacts with the West
    d. rebuild the Chinese army

13. The Great Leap Forward:
    a. ended in failure.
    b. led to a massive famine in China.
    c. led Mao to cede power to Chou En-lai.
    d. all of the above.

14. After Mao's death his wife:
    a. took power.
    b. was tried for crimes against the state.
    c. became China's foreign minister.
    d. went into exile in North Korea.

15. In 1978, two years after Mao's death, power was peacefully passed to:
    a. Chiang Ch'ing.
    b. Teng Hsiao-p'ing.
    c. Chou En-lai.
    d. Liu Hsiao-ch'i.

16. Since 1988 Taiwan has:
    a. become more democratic.
    b. had poor diplomatic relations with Japan.
    c. has grown more repressive.
    d. increasingly anti-communist in its rhetoric.

CHAPTER 18
Korea and Southeast Asia in the Modern World

Outline Of Main Ideas

A. Yi Dynasty Korea in Decline
- tributary relations with China—Korea's "elder brother"; a hereditary hierarchy implanted on a Confucian socio-political system; the yangban or gentry class
- the Yi Dynasty weakened by rival factions; Hideyoshi's invasions; the Manchu conquests; cultural and economic weakness; Korea ill-prepared to face the Western threat

i. Rejection of Foreign Ideas
- rigid rejection of the West; the persecution of Catholics; Korea—the battleground for Russian, Chinese and Japanese imperialism; Western learning spreads via Christianity; the conservative backlash; the Tonghak ("Eastern Learning") Movement; the restoration of the Yi under Taewongun ("Grand Prince"); Korean dependence on China

ii. Foreign Contention for Korea
- Japan opens Korea; Korea's anti-foreign response; China takes control of Korean affairs and the political power of the conservative Min Family; Japanese involvement in Korean affairs and the Japanese-led coup; the Tonghak Rebellion; the Sino-Japanese War (1895); Korea as a Japanese sphere of influence; the Russo-Japanese War (1905); Korea as a Japanese protectorate; Japanese suppression

B. Korea Under Japanese Rule
   - severe Japanese domination and exploitation; the rise of Korean nationalism; the spread of Christianity and its influence; the foundation of the Korean Communist Party

C. Division and War
   - the end of World War II; Korea divided at the 38th parallel into North and South Korea; the North Korean invasion; the United Nations resolution; the Korean War: MacArthur and China, MacArthur and Truman, the destruction and overall impact of the war on Koreans

D. Korea Since 1960
   - South Korean agriculture and industry, North Korean raw materials; Korea unnaturally divided; rapid Southern development, relatively stunted Northern development
   - South Korea: Syngman Rhee; Park; Chun; Roh; Kim; government institutions and policy; the rising middle class; Korean use of the Japanese model of economic development
   - North Korea: Kim Il Sung and his successor; hostility across the 38th parallel

E. Southeast Asia Since World War II
   - adoption of the Chinese model of revolution by Southeast Asian nationalist groups; the failure of colonial rule to produce a viable democratic alternative to Chinese socialism

F. Vietnam
   - Vietnam's historical cultural relations with China; cultural ties to Southeast Asia; Vietnamese expansion south; the spread of Christianity; French control; brutal and exploitative French rule; Ho Chi Minh and the Comintern; the Japanese invasion ends French domination

   i. Vietnam's Thirty Years of War
      - the Viet Minh and the Democratic Republic of Vietnam; the French and U.S. reconquest of Vietnam; communist guerrilla warfare against French rule; Chinese support; Dien Bien Phu and Vietnam's defeat of France

- the Geneva Conference and partition of Vietnam; Diem and U.S. commitment to South Vietnam; the National Liberation Front; TET; the ruthless war; the reversal of U.S. public opinion; U.S. bombings and withdrawal
- Results of the war: tremendous devastation; the power of Vietnamese nationalism; the cost of the war; the U.S. responses to the war; the U.S. embargo

G. Bloody Cambodia
- from French colonialism to independence; Prince Sihanouk; Lon Nol; the secret U.S. bombings of Cambodia; the rise of Pol Pot and his Khmer Rouge; vicious and irrational social engineering and Cambodia's holocaust; Vietnamese intervention (1979); Vietnamese withdrawal (1989); UN intervention and elections

H. Laos: The Forgotten Country
- the Japanese occupation; U.S. aid to noncommunists; the civil war; U.S. bombings and the rise of the communists; exclusive social policies; poverty

I. Burma, Thailand, Malaya, and Singapore

   i. Burma
   - the Japanese occupation; the Anti-Fascist People's Freedom League (AFPFL); Aung San; U Nu: Burmese independence (1948); rebellion; Ne Win; the police state; international isolation; National League; Suu Kyi

   ii. Thailand
   - the Japanese occupation; Thailand-U.S. relations and the Vietnam War; military rule; the Thai monarchy; the democratic movement and its suppression; economic development

   iii. Malaya and Singapore
   - the Japanese occupation; the Chinese minority; The Emergency; communist insurrection; Malayan independence (1957); Singapore; Borneo; the Malay-Chinese conflict; the parliamentary system; economic development
   - Singapore: economic development; Lee Kuan Yew, one-party rule

J. Indonesia
- the Japanese occupation; Sukarno and Hatta; Dutch reoccupation of Indonesia; Indonesian independence (1949)
- tremendous geographical diversity; Bahasa Indonesian (national language); the communist and Sukarno alliance; General Suharto's anti-communist coup and suppression (1965); the police state; anti-Chinese discrimination; uneven economic growth

K. The Philippines
- the Japanese occupation; Filipino independence (1946); U.S. anti-communism; culture: Spain and the U.S.; the Huk Rebellion; Magsaysay and the defeat of the rebels; Marcos rule: corruption, rebellion, the assassination of Benigno Aquino, the election of Corazon Aquino; social problems; Ramos

Essay And Discussion Questions

1. Modern Korean history has proven to be remarkably tumultuous. Why is that the case?
The geographic location and relatively small size of Korea has placed it at a tremendous disadvantage in the scheme of world events. In 19th and early 20th century geopolitics, Korea sat at the nexus between the major Asian powers China, Japan, and Russia. As these giants sought to expand their respective spheres of influence in Asia, Korean soil became a natural battleground due to its strategic location. During the Cold War period, a divided Korea became the boundary between the Soviet Union and the United States. In virtually all of Korea's many modern conflicts, the Korean people have had external events shape their nation's destiny and have become pawns in a much larger geopolitical games.

Korea's internal affairs, however, have also shaped the road. Korea's willingness to depend on Chinese support and defense meant that the it did not formulate a coherent or effective foreign policy until the Western powers and Japan had already become far too powerful to deal with on an equal basis. Korea's early and rigid rejection of the West and exceptionally conservative court served the same purpose: wasting valuable time hoping that the foreigners would disappear. By the time the court realized their hopes were in vain, they had lost the opportunity for initiative.

2. Why did Maoist communism become the model of choice among Southeast Asian nationalists after World War II? Why did no moderate alternatives rival the communists?

   While many might promote communist social programs or ideology as the major attraction of the Maoist model of revolution, the fact remains that the Mao's strategy proved successful beyond all others at resisting and eventually overthrowing a much stronger political opponent. Mao's triumph inspired nationalists facing similar circumstances in other countries all over the globe.

   One of the more impressive elements of the Maoist model was its ability to survive and actually thrive under adverse or hostile conditions. Under colonial rule nationalist organizations faced considerable pressure from the police and other enforcement agencies. Moderate groups generally tried to work "within the system" by lobbying for new laws, and greater freedom within the colonial government system. However, rather than bringing about reform, such measures only angered colonial leaders who jailed, assassinated and "purged" the moderate nationalist groups using police and other enforcement agencies. Those moderate nationalists able to survive the onslaught could in no way continue their efforts at moderate reform for fear of generating further backlash. Under such conditions, moderate elements were forced to abandon their nationalist efforts or become radicals.

   Over time, virtually all nationalists advocating democracy or other middle-road, moderate reform found themselves in jail or suppressed to the point that they became impotent. Only radical groups working underground could survive. When the Japanese arrived, these groups flourished by engaging in anti-Japanese guerrilla warfare and organizational development. By the time the Japanese left, the popularity and political power of these radical groups had increased many fold.

3. Why did France and then the United States return to Vietnam after World War II instead of granting it independence?

   World War II proved to be particularly embarrassing to the French. After surrendering early to Hitler and then collaborating with him and the Japanese in Indochina, France emerged from the war on the winning side but with little cause to boast. Damaged national prestige needed a cause for celebration, not another failure. No French government could face the prospect of waving goodbye to France's colonies in Indochina without a fight. Eager to restore France's pre-war glory, post-war Frenchmen roared back into Vietnam in an effort to reassert colonial rule. What they found, however, proved that the clock could not be turned back, nor the status quo regained.

The United States initially resisted France's return to Indochina, but eventually agreed in order to press France to play a stronger role in the defense of Europe against the perceived Soviet threat. Later, however, when it appeared that communism had begun its march through Asia, the U.S. reversed its opposition and committed support to the French cause. By the time of Dien Bien Phu in 1954, the Cold War had reached full gear and concerns that the spread of communism would continue unless actively stopped motivated Washington's commitment of supplies and troops to the area.

Questions For Class Discussion

1. What are the reasons for the successful establishment and growth of Christianity within Korea?
   Originally, Christianity faced roughly the same prospects for success as in China or Japan. However, with the Japanese invasion, the religion came to be associated with the resistance movement. Tied to nationalism, the popularity of the religion spread even as the Japanese tried to stamp it out.

2. Do you agree with the author's assertion that it would have been better to accept "a unified Communist Korea [in order to avoid] the massive destruction suffered and the legacy of division and tension?"
   Either argument should mention the war itself and the failure of democracy on both sides of the peninsula. The middle class of the South, with its material well-being will also be a major point to be contended with. The issue likely to be raised in disagreement with the author is that most recently South Korea has shown a strong stable economy with a growing democracy, whereas the North's economy is collapsing, causing extreme hardships for most citizens and no prospect of democracy. Relative freedom in the south might also be compared with rigid social control in the north.

3. Compare and explain the major differences between the independence movements of Vietnam and India.
   Though both movements started in earnest at roughly the same time (India 1920, Vietnam 1925-30), Vietnam's began after a much shorter period of Western colonial

rule. The differences in the total number of years is largely due to two factors. First, the French began their rule as oppressive exploiters, whereas British rule in India only became so after eighty years or so. Both powers engaged in the more extreme abuse during the same time period due to the rise of Social Darwinism in Europe during the late 1800s. Secondly, Vietnam is more homogeneous and geographically much smaller than India. Thus it was easier for Vietnamese nationalists to unify the people to common cause. Finally, another obvious difference is that after World War II, Britain realized the new situation in Asia and withdrew while France did not and continued with its imperialist policies.

4. Most of Southeast Asia's newly independent states have had immense difficulty expanding their economies. Yet others, such as Singapore and Thailand have been very successful. What are the major reasons for the differences? (Taiwan and/or India are also appropriate for this question.)
Education is one key reason. The British in Singapore provided more education than any other colonial power in Southeast Asia. Thailand's education system, though not strong, was at least available for the upper class. The rest did not provide education. The countries that did succeed were also granted some level of colonial rule by the native peoples. Thailand of course was never completely colonized. This gave invaluable experience to scores of individual in running governments and businesses, whereas generations of people in the other nations did not gain that experience. The example of Indonesia is a good counter-example.

5. What arguments might Indonesian leaders use against allowing greater democratization?
Indonesia is similar to India in that it is a "hodgepodge of different ethnic, religious, and linguistic groups." This makes democracy very difficult. For example, when Indonesia was newly independent, village chiefs in the regions farthest from Jakarta ignored the central government. When the military-style leaders came into power the government became much more centralized. Students might also point out the economic success Indonesia has had, especially compared to neighbors such as Cambodia, Burma, and others.

Multiple Choice Questions

1. The Eastern Learning movement was directed against:
   a. Chinese and Japanese influence.
   b. the weak Yi government and Western influence.
   c. the urban middle class.
   d. the Grand Prince and his Japanese advisors.

2. In 1876 Japan:
   a. made Korea into a dependent state.
   b. conquered Korea.
   c. forced Korea to open its ports to Japanese trade.
   d. annexed the southern part of Korea.

3. Throughout much of the nineteenth century Korean relations with the outside world was handled by:
   a. the Japanese.
   b. China.
   c. the military.
   d. the Buddhist priesthood.

4. After 1895 Korea fell under the influence of:
   a. China.
   b. Manchuria.
   c. Russia.
   d. Japan.

5. Between 1910 and 1945 Japan's policy toward Korea was to:
   a. treat it as an equal.
   b. exploit it and repress Korean culture.
   c. modernize it.
   d. prepare its people for self-government.

6. Under the Japanese, public education in Korea:
   a. became mandatory for all Koreans.
   b. emphasized Korean language and history.
   c. taught Japanese.
   d. prepared Koreans to assume government positions in the colonial government.

7. The Chinese intervened in the Korean War to:
   a. protect their northeast border.
   b. protect Russian interest in Korea.
   c. conquer Korea for itself.
   d. to prepare for the conquest of Japan.

8. Since 1960 South Korea has:
   a. become a democracy.
   b. reunited with the North.
   c. become an industrial power.
   d. stagnated.

9. Since WWII, probably the most stable nation in Southeast Asia has been:
   a. Cambodia.
   b. Indonesia.
   c. Burma.
   d. Thailand.

10. The leader of the nationalist movement in Vietnam was:
    a. Bao Dai.
    b. Ho Chi Minh.
    c. Ngo Dinh Diem.
    d. General Giap.

11. The Vietnamese decisively defeated the French at the Battle of:
    a. Hue City.
    b. Khe Sanh.
    c. Dien Bien Phu.
    d. the A Drang Valley.

12. The Ho Chi Minh Trail:
    a. ran through Laos and Cambodia.
    b. supplied Communist troops in South Vietnam.
    c. was a key element in the Vietnam War against the U.S.
    d. was all of the above.

13. Communism in Cambodia has been:
    a. less severe than in Vietnam.
    b. virtually genocidal.
    c. greatly influenced by Russia.
    d. disorganized to the point of having little impact.

14. The Khmer Rouge are:
    a. Vietnamese Communists.
    b. a branch of the Red Guards.
    c. Chinese volunteers who fought in Vietnam.
    d. Cambodian Communists.

15. The leader of the Burmese independence movement was:
    a. U Nu.
    b. Aung San.
    c. U Thant.
    d. Ne Win.

16. Throughout most of the last twenty years Burma has:
    a. been involved in a bloody civil war.
    b. isolated itself from the world.
    c. been in the midst of massive modernization.
    d. been a dependency of India.

17. The leader of the current reform movement in Burma is:
    a. Suu Kyi.
    b. Son Bot.
    c. Ne Win.
    d. U Nu.

18. The Chinese population of Thailand has been:
    a. isolated from the native population.
    b. heavily persecuted.
    c. completely assimilated.
    d. expelled.

19. The population of Singapore is largely:
    a. Chinese.
    b. Indonesian.
    c. Malayan.
    d. Indian.

20. The leader of the independence movement in Indonesia was:
    a. Suharto.
    b. Mantak Chi.
    c. Sukarno.
    d. Dunh Khor.

21. Which of the following people has not been elected as president of the Philippines?
    a. Ferdinand Marcos
    b. Corazon Aquino
    c. Ramon Magasaysay
    d. Emilio Aguinaldo

CHAPTER 19
South Asia: Independence, Political Division, and Development

Outline Of Main Ideas
- South Asian states and peoples; British colonialism; nationalism and independence; Churchill's defeat in the British elections
- desires of the Muslim League for an independent Muslim state; fears of Hindu domination; political ambitions served by violence; Mountbatten and the English withdrawal; late British concessions and India's partition

A. Partition
   - independence of a separate India and Pakistan; massive migration and violence
   - Pakistan: the brain drain of educated Hindus and floods of Muslim refugees, severed cultural, business, and transportation links

   i. The Kashmir Conflict
   - the problem of Kashmir; a Hindu ruler over a Muslim majority; war; the division of Kashmir between India and Pakistan; Gandhi's failure and assassination

B. Bangladesh and Pakistan
   - East Pakistan's isolation and neglect; military government control; elections and success of the East Pakistan Party; West Pakistan's failed attempt to quash the Party; the emergence of an independent East Pakistan—now Bangladesh; Bangladesh problems: murder, assassination, instability, high population growth rates, poor economy, flooding, deforestation
   - West Pakistan: ineffective leadership and martial law; General Ayub and competent administration: economic and national planning, agriculture; the rise of General

Yahya Khan, Zulfikar Ali Bhutto and Zia-ul-Huq; the spread of corruption, cronyism, and favoritism; Pakistan and the Afghan rebels; Pakistan—the U.S. Cold War client; U.S. military supplies in Pakistan; the failure of identifying a national purpose; Benazir Bhutto and her opposition; government weakness and U.S. withdrawal of support; war with India; the paramilitary government; Bhutto's return

C. Afghanistan
- a buffer between British India and Russian Central Asia; fierce Islamic tribes; the Soviet sponsored Afghan government and civil war; Soviet withdrawal and the government's survival; national fragmentation, poverty, and lost resources

D. Sri Lanka
- independence despite a weak nationalistic movement; "second wave" nationalism; "Ceylon Tamils," "Indian Tamils," and the Sinhalese; Bandaranaike; Indian troops in Sri Lanka; agriculture; industry; modern services; civil war and terrorism

E. Nepal
- a British protectorate; the Gurkhas; the monarchy; slow modernization and poverty; erosion; the Himalayas and tourism; ties with India and China; King Bihendra

F. India After Independence
- thriving democracy; Nehru and Indian federalism; the states; Hindi as the national language; English as an associate language; southern resentment of "northern domination"

   i. India Under Nehru
   - industrial economic development and handicrafts; traditional rural councils; expanding cities and their problems; India's growing population; social stratification and uneven distribution of wealth; border disputes with China; Pan-Asianism and nonalignment; Nehru's death; Indira Gandhi

    ii. India Under Indira Gandhi
- the voting public and its interest in politics; India's commitment to democracy; the green revolution; industrial growth; further stratification; the national emergency of June, 1975; Indira Gandhi's defeat at the polls and her subsequent success; India's high tech performance and modernization

    iii. The Sikhs
- the Sikhs and their relative prosperity under the green revolution; rising expectations and dissatisfaction with the government; Indira Gandhi's inflexibility and assassination

    iv. Indira Gandhi's Successors
- Rajiv Gandhi's flexible leadership; voter dissatisfaction and V.P. Singh; Hindu-Muslim violence in Kashmir; the Untouchables; student violence; Hindu-Muslim tension; Singh's defeat; the assassination of Rajiv Gandhi; Rao and economic growth

    v. India Today
- poverty, population pressures, and communal division; nationalism and the problem of creating an "Indian identity"; positive economic growth in India (relative to China); unequal distribution of wealth; India's poverty and the stages of economic development (vis-à-vis the Western experience); relative deprivation and positive economic trends

    vi. Women Leaders of South Asia
- the prominence of women; the Keralan exception to female subjugation; Sirimavo Bandaranaike; Indira Gandhi

G. Indian and South Asian Achievements and Shortcomings
- the economy, natural resources: oil; transportation

    i. Changing Perceptions of Caste and Ethnicity
- iron and the Parsees; Indian entrepreneurs and Hinduism; the caste system and economic growth; caste and political power; the decline of caste; education

ii. Rural Development
   - rural poverty despite strides in development; other rural problems; water and irrigation; uneven growth and development; cattle veneration and the "white revolution"; diet; discrimination

  iii. Some Threats to Development
   - deforestation, soil erosion, and soil exhaustion; urban pollution; the Union Carbide disaster; population growth and controls; the demand for more children; education; migration of peasants to urban areas

Essay And Discussion Questions

1. Why has the United States supported Pakistan, with its totalitarian government, rather than India with its democratic system?
During the Cold War, the United States cast about looking for allies against the Soviet Union and its consortium of allies. While NATO (North Atlantic Treaty Organization) and the Warsaw Pact were ostensibly divided between nations honoring democracy and those committed to communism respectively, in many areas of the world the lines blurred, depending not on a particular nation's democratic or communist commitments so much as its connections to Moscow or Washington. In fact, many nations played the two sides to their own advantage, drawing resources from both the Soviets and the U.S.

India and Pakistan are a good case. India preferred "nonalliance," refusing to establish binding ties with either side so as to preserve its own policy-making sovereignty and independence. Indians recognized clearly that alignment would involve foreigners in its own affairs and possible get India dragged into a war. Thus, Indian leaders spurned offers extended by both the superpowers.

Pakistan, on the other hand, had few qualms with alignment because it offered so many opportunities to the resource-poor nation. With a close U.S. alignment, Pakistan could avoid heavy military expenditures, get lots of money and weapons that could be used against India if the need arise, and obtain promises of backing from Washington should the Soviets have decided to press south into their territory.

The U.S., meanwhile, chose to align with Pakistan, first because the Indians rejected an alliance while Pakistan sought just such an alliance; secondly because Pakistan's location near the old Soviet empire and China made it a perfect first line of defense against communist aggression into South Asia; and third, because if the U.S. didn't align with Pakistan, then the Soviets certainly would have.

2. How did the caste system fare in India's new democratic system?
Many Western observers felt that the lines of distinction between different castes would make it difficult to execute the democratic process. However, even as it declines, the caste system has in some ways girded up the democratic system in India. Individuals coming from traditional Indian society already possessed a group consciousness associated with the caste system and its institutions and organizations that easily transferred to political activism or interest groups eager to participate in the democratic process. In some cases, particularly among the Untouchables and low status castes, caste members have formed political parties to represent them and have won benefits and other advantages that had previously been denied.

3. What are the reasons that more traditionally minded families, particularly in rural areas, still prefer to have many rather than few children?
Like most Asian countries, India has not yet produced any effective or satisfactory system for caring for the elderly that can presently compete with the security traditionally offered by the family. Most elderly have either been unable or unwilling to save and accumulate resources for use in their old age. And, even if they did, depending upon their children for sustenance proves much more comforting and attractive than any institution staffed with strangers. In addition, even when the children are still quite young, their labor contributes to the overall cash flow of the family. In short, the more children one has, the more resources at one's disposal while they are young and the more resources available to one in old-age.

Questions For Class Discussion

1. Compare the writings of Nehru (Box 19-1) and Sjahrir (Box 18-5).
Both men were Western educated and feel more at home with Western culture and thought. They tended to be worried about the current state of their native lands and concerned about the future.

2. Great Britain is still generally well regarded by most Indians. Why might that be?
The "positives" were covered in previous chapters (13 and 14). If your students compare British rule to that of the French and Dutch (Chapters 16 and 18) the British

were much more humane. Is Britain to blame for the violence associated with the actual partition of India? Did the British leaders realize the problems their delay in giving India its independence would cause? The evidence indicates that they did not. Many find it difficult to place the blame on Britain. If so even Gandhi could be painted with the same brush for he himself stopped political action for five years (1924-29, Chapter 16). If he had continued the pressure, Britain might have "quit India" sooner.

3. Given the long precedent of division and regionalism in India's history, was the partition a "vivisection?"
An immediate answer might be "no, partition was inevitable" since throughout almost all of Indian history, India had not been a centralized state but rather separate kingdoms. Even during times of dynastic rule, most regions maintained broad levels of autonomy. The issue becomes more complicated when one considers that the advent of technology made it much easier for a centralized government to control its outer regions and the rise of "Indian" nationalism during the 1920's and 1930's gave most Indians a vision of a united India. If India had been granted independence before 1939 it may have indeed survived without partition, as suggested by Professor Murphey.

4. How have the struggles facing the South Asian states of India, Pakistan, and Bangladesh since independence shown similarities?
All three have had problems with minorities wishing to secede from their country, including the Kashmir and Punjab regions of India, the war between the Tamils and Sinhalese in Sri Lanka and the successful break of Bangladesh from Pakistan. Pakistan continues to have problems: the Punjab area and the land inhabited by Baluchis have made noises of independence.

All three have also had problems with overpopulation. India's population of 900 million is expected to surpass China within forty years, and India still has not successfully addressed population control. In addition, all three (along with many other nations) face serious environmental problems. Along with the usual air pollution and smog of the big cities, South Asia is dealing with the effects of deforestation. Where much of the population uses wood for cooking and heat, the stripping of forests (even from city parks) has caused very serious soil erosion. This is most prominent in Bangladesh, where the deforestation in China, India, and Bangladesh along the Bramaputra River has led to serious flooding in the delta region.

5. "The liberation of women was one of the goals of the [Chinese] Revolution" and of the Indian National Congress. How successful have these countries (compared or individually) been in meeting this goal?
China has made "considerable progress" (Chapter 17) but is still far behind the West. The same is true for India. The biggest change is seen in the city. However, matrimonial ads from parents or older brothers still advertise women with Ph.D.'s who are in their thirties and cannot find spouses.

6. Does the women's movement in Asia today represent real progress, or is it simply another example of the imperialistic imposition of Western morays on other cultures?
Many think that it was wrong for the West to impose Western culture on the colonies. It is often felt that language, dress styles, religion, and school curriculum should reflect native culture in a positive way. If cultural imposition such as this smacks of imperialism, or even an element of Social Darwinism, does not demanding Western standards of "progress" in women's rights constitute the same sort of demand? There are many Western groups that go to Asian countries and encourage women to change (similar to missionaries?) or even ask their Western countries to punish Asian governments that do not "progress" in the field of human rights fast enough. Of course, there is no answer to this question. It is just food for thought.

7. What might lead the author to conclude that "India will not break up into warring factions or regional conflict?" Do you share in his optimism? Why?
(This question may also be used in Chapter 20.) India's recent problems include conflicts in Kashmir, Punjab, and Assam along with continued fighting between groups of Hindus and Muslims. There certainly is "promise" for the future as India's economy continues to grow. The populace is well educated and the peasant class is better fed and has more opportunity than ever before. Also, the first fifty years are generally considered the most difficult for a new government and India has survived its first half century intact.

Multiple Choice Questions

1. The founder of modern Pakistan was:
   a. Ali Bhutto.
   b. Ayub Khan.
   c. Ali Jinnah.
   d. Yahya Khan.

2. Which of the following was *not* a factor leading to the partition of India in 1947?
    a. The ambitions of Muslim politicians
    b. The ambitions of Muslim merchants in Karachi
    c. Strong INC support for partition
    d. British delays in granting freedom to India

3. Winston Churchill:
    a. supported Indian independence.
    b. opposed Indian independence.
    c. was indifferent to India.
    d. thought India was no longer of value to England.

4. The major source of conflict between India and Pakistan is:
    a. control of the waters of the Indus.
    b. Indian treatment of Moslems.
    c. control of Kashmir.
    d. the border of Punjab and India.

5. The leader of the independence movement in Bangladesh which separated Bangladesh from Pakistan was:
    a. Ayub Khan.
    b. Sheik Mujib.
    c. Ali Pasha.
    d. Benazir Bhutto.

6. Ali Bhutto was deposed as president of Pakistan and put to death by:
    a. Ali Jinnah.
    b. Yahya Khan.
    c. Sheik Mujbur Rahman.
    d. Zia-ul-Huq.

7. Throughout the late 1970s and early 1980s Afghanistan was at war with:
    a. China.
    b. Iran.
    c. the Soviet Union.
    d. Pakistan.

8. Sri Lanka is beset by ethnic conflict between the Sinhalese majority and the:
   a. Hindi minority.
   b. Muslim minority.
   c. Tamil minority.
   d. Hmong minority.

9. Which of the following figures was never Prime Minister of India?
   a. Jawarlahal Nehru
   b. Mahatma Gandhi
   c. Lal Shastri
   d. Rajiv Gandhi

10. Under the rule of Indira Gandhi, India did all of the following except:
    a. modernize India's agriculture.
    b. declare martial law and suppress the press.
    c. complete a nuclear test.
    d. fight a war with China.

11. One problem that Indira Gandhi was unable to overcome was:
    a. Sikh unrest.
    b. agricultural production.
    c. Tamil insurgence.
    d. maintaining good relations with the West.

12. Which of the following Indian politicians was not assassinated?
    a. Indira Gandhi
    b. Jawarlahal Nehru
    c. Rajiv Gandhi
    d. Mahatma Gandhi

13. Which of the following women has never been a ruler of a South Asian country?
    a. Benazir Bhutto
    b. Indira Gandhi
    c. Suu Kyi
    d. Sirimavo Bandaranaike

14. The Gurka troops of the British army come from:
    a. India.
    b. Nepal.
    c. Sri Lanka.
    d. Bangladesh.

CHAPTER 20
Asia at the Close of the Century

Outline Of Main Ideas
- signs of violence; population growth and material prosperity; the third world and Asia; poverty and relative deprivation; poverty and social problems; communism and nationalism; nationalism and violence; wealthy stable Asian nations verses poor unstable Asian nations; present material prosperity and economic growth; Asia's broad spectrum of political systems

A. Population Growth
   - Asia's population and its ratio to resources; environmental problems; population control measures; high birth rates except in Taiwan, Japan and Singapore; the relationship between old age security and children; social conditions for lowering birth rates

B. Pollution
   - economic growth and environmental pollution; automobiles; China's heavy utilization of coal and urban pollution

C. Urbanization
   - growth and opportunity in urban areas; immigration; high population density; the lure of the city; stages of development and Asian cities; extraordinary pollution problems; rising expectations and changes in the rural countryside; the Japanese model of pollution control

D. Economic Growth Rates
- Asia's record breaking economic growth rates; China's progress; high economic growth rates and "Confucian" culture: education, work ethic, family support; Western verses Eastern education

E. Tradition in Modern Asia
- Asian pride in its heritage; Asian technological development and Europe's use of it; Asian complacency; Western arrogance and conquest of Asia; Asian cultural pride; the requirements of modernity and Asia's traditional heritage; short-lived Western dominance; the resurgence of Asian nationalisms and independence; programs for modernity

F. A Country-by-Country Survey

  i. India
  - India's continued use of traditional symbols; Gandhi's reliance on Hindu symbols for modern purposes: non-violence; traditional symbols today; the caste system and India's modernization; Indian nativism; speculation about the future

  ii. China
  - Chinese rejection of culture and heritage; Lu Hsun's critique of government corruption; the Kuomintang's failure to address social issues; China's humiliation at the hands of Westerners; the communist takeover and Chinese pride; attacks on traditional Chinese culture; Mao's vision of a bright, new dawn; disaster in the Great Leap and the Cultural Revolution; renewed interest in China's heritage; Chinese efforts to find a balance between tradition and modernity

  iii. Japan
  - Japan's preservation of its traditional culture despite modernization; initial temptations to abandon traditional culture; traditional culture as a source of pride and security in times of transformation and uncertainty

  iv. Southeast Asia and Korea
  - Southeast Asian tradition and identity; new forms of colonialism; the agrarian nature of Southeast Asia and its dependence on foreign capital; second-wave

nationalism; Buddhism in Burma; Tagalog in the Philippines; Korean, Mongolian and Tibetan efforts to assert tradition

Essay And Discussion Questions

1. What connections can be drawn between East Asia's high economic growth rates and its Confucian heritage?

   During the 1920s, Confucianism and the Confucian system that dominated East Asia for over two thousand years came to be viewed by many Chinese intellectuals and leaders as an obstacle to modernization and the primary cause of China's relative backwardness vis-à-vis the Western powers and Japan. From the May Fourth Movement to the Cultural Revolution, these individuals sharply denounced Confucius and implemented political campaigns to erase the Confucian influence from China. Similar policies could be found in North Korea and later in Vietnam.

   Meanwhile, within the free societies of Taiwan, Japan, Singapore, Hong Kong and South Korea, Confucianism adapted itself to the modern world. The age-old Confucian emphasis on education and its role in transforming society naturally reinforced these countries' modern education systems, producing some of the world's most literate and competent work forces. Contrast this to China where the Cultural Revolution and other political campaigns hampered or dissolved the educational system.

   Confucianism's emphasis on the family and family unity has also aided modernization by helping East Asia avoid social problems such as disaffected youth, divorce and social alienation. Families tended to become self-sufficient and support family members as well as sanctioning socially unacceptable behavior, thus helping to keep crime at relatively low levels. Also, the hierarchical, group-oriented, social system associated with Confucian culture, with its attendant loyalty has allowed many of these nations to formulate national economic plans and work towards them in a rational manner and avoid the fits and starts facing more individualistic countries (such as India).

2. In what ways does the promotion and celebration of traditional culture help smooth the rough transition from traditional to modern society?

   One of the greatest trials a society trying to modernize must face involves the dislocation and dissolution of the traditional institutions or beliefs that rooted people and gave them their identity and security. The problem becomes particularly acute when the modern equivalents to these traditional institutions have not yet adequately formed. For example, individuals leaving the farm, with its associated family, village, religious or caste ties, with its security and support, and with its familiarity, may find themselves isolated and vulnerable when they go to work in a factory, with its loud and intimidating machinery and surrounding cityscape that looks more Western than Asian.

Traditional culture tends to ameliorate this culture shock by holding out familiar symbols, such as the spinning wheel, which act as a reminder of who the people really are—"We are not Indians simply trying to imitate Western culture and industry, but Indians ushering in a modern India." Traditional culture also connects individuals to the past by giving them a heritage to which they belong. Such links to the past and "mother India" or "T'ang China and her glory" helped the self-esteem of the nation as well, particularly since the experience of many Asian nations with European domination tainted modernization as "imperialist." Retaining traditional culture also binds a people together while delineating them from their enemies--thus it serves nationalistic objectives as well.

Naturally, however, traditional culture itself must be modernized. Some parts never adapt—such as foot binding in China—and those that do are seldom fully reflect their traditional manifestation. In a word, traditional culture in a modern society ceases to be "traditional" but becomes "national" instead.

Questions For Class Discussion

1. Now that you have finished the course, how would you answer the question, "Why study Asia (or the country/region covered)?"

Multiple Choice Questions

1. Which of the following could be considered a "Third World" country
   a. Chinese and Japanese influence.
   b. the weak Yi government and Western influence.
   c. the urban middle class.
   d. the Grand Prince and his Japanese advisors.

2. Probably the single most important factor in the rising population of Asia is:
   a. lack of wars.
   b. increased life expectancy.
   c. birth control.
   d. industrialization.

3. Which of the following Asian countries has a democratic government?
   a. Indonesia
   b. China
   c. Vietnam
   d. India

4. Which of the following has *not* been a problem caused by deforestation in Asia?
   a. Floods
   b. Erosion
   c. Fires
   d. Choked rivers

5. It seems to be a general rule of population growth that:
   a. birth rates go down as incomes increase.
   b. birth rates fall as incomes decrease.
   c. city dwellers have more children than farmers.
   d. as cities grow, birth rates rise.

6. Although many countries in Asia have high economic growth rates, this growth has not kept pace with:
   a. that of the rest of the world.
   b. food production.
   c. population growth.
   d. the growth of South America.

ANSWER SECTION

Introduction
1. B
2. C
3. D
4. A
5. C
6. D
7. A

Chapter 1
1. A
2. C
3. C
4. D
5. A
6. B
7. B
8. A
9. D
10. B
11. C
12. B
13. D

Chapter 2
1. D
2. B
3. A

4. C
5. D
6. B
7. C
8. B
9. C
10. D
11. B
12. C
13. D
14. A
15. A
16. A
17. C
18. B
19. B
20. A
21. B
22. D
23. D
24. B

Chapter 3
1. A
2. D
3. C
4. D
5. B

6. C
7. A
8. B
9. B
10. C
11. D
12. C
13. B
14. A
15. C
16. D
17. B
18. B
19. C

Chapter 4
1. B
2. D
3. A
4. B
5. C
6. A
7. A
8. C
9. B
10. C
11. A
12. D
13. C
14. A
15. D

Chapter 5
1. B
2. A
3. B
4. B

5. D
6. C
7. C
8. B
9. A
10. D
11. B
12. C
13. A

Chapter 6
1. D
2. D
3. B
4. D
5. B
6. C
7. A
8. B
9. C
10. A
11. B
12. C
13. C
14. B
15. C
16. C
17. C
18. B

Chapter 7
1. C
2. A
3. B
4. C
5. B
6. B

7. C
8. D
9. C
10. C

Chapter 8
1. C
2. B
3. A
4. C
5. C
6. C
7. D
8. C
9. C
10. B
11. A
12. A
13. A
14. C
15. B
16. C
17. C
18. B
19. C

Chapter 9
1. B
2. C
3. C
4. C
5. A
6. D
7. C
8. B
9. B
10. B

11. D
12. C
13. D

Chapter 10
1. B
2. A
3. D
4. C
5. D
6. C
7. A
8. B
9. B
10. C

Chapter 11
1. B
2. C
3. D
4. D
5. C
6. C
7. B
8. A
9. A
10. C
11. D
12. C
13. D
14. B
15. C
16. B
17. C
18. D
19. C
20. B

21. A
22. C
23. B

Chapter 12
1. C
2. C
3. C
4. C
5. B
6. C
7. B
8. C
9. D
10. C
11. B
12. C

Chapter 13
1. C
2. A
3. D
4. C
5. D
6. C
7. C
8. C
9. D
10. A
11. D
12. D
13. A
14. D
15. B
16. C
17. D
18. A

19. B
20. D
21. C
22. B
23. B
24. C

Chapter 14
1. C
2. A
3. A
4. C
5. A
6. C
7. B
8. D
9. D
10. C
11. D
12. C
13. D
14. B
15. B
16. D
17. C
18. C
19. D
20. C
21. C
22. B
23. D

Chapter 15
1. A
2. C
3. A
4. B

5. B
6. C
7. B
8. A
9. C
10. D
11. B
12. B
13. C
14. A
15. C
16. B
17. B
18. B
19. D

Chapter 16
1. C
2. D
3. B
4. A
5. C
6. C
7. D
8. B
9. B
10. D
11. B
12. D
13. B
14. C
15. B
16. C
17. A
18. A

Chapter 17
1. A
2. D
3. B
4. C
5. D
6. C
7. B
8. C
9. B
10. D
11. B
12. B
13. D
14. B
15. B
16. A

Chapter 18
1. B
2. C
3. B
4. D
5. B
6. C
7. A
8. C
9. D
10. B
11. C
12. D
13. B
14. D
15. B
16. B
17. A
18. C

19. A
20. C
21. D

Chapter 19
1. C
2. C
3. B
4. C
5. B
6. D
7. C
8. C
9. B

10. D
11. A
12. B
13. C
14. B

Chapter 20
1. C
2. B
3. D
4. C
5. A
6. C